DEVELOP YOUR INTUITION

AND PSYCHIC POWERS

DAVID FURLONG

DEVELOP YOUR INTUITION
AND PSYCHIC POWERS

New Skills for Changing Times

ATLANTA

BOOKS

To Claire, Maaten, Abe and Lily

I wish to express my sincere appreciation for all the help and support that I have received in the preparation of this book. In particular I thank my students, friends and colleagues who have been subjected to the different exercises that have been included here and whose valuable responses have provided the basis for this training. I would like to acknowledge the late Bob Morris, the Koestler Professor of Parapsychology at the University of Edinburgh, for information on parapsychological research projects and Jayne Hall for helping revise this present edition.

Finally, I would like to thank HA and my many guides and helpers from the 'Quantum Realm', without whose inspiration this book would never have been completed.

First published 1996 by Bloomsbury Publishing Plc, 2 Soho Square, London W1V 6HB

This edition 2008 by Atlanta Books, Myrtles, Como Road, Malvern, Worcs WR14 2TH

ISBN 978-0-9559795-0-7

A copy of the CIP entry for this book is available from the British Library

Contents

Foreword

A dozen years have passed since the first edition of this book and in that time we have seen some dramatic changes in the field of personal technology. The internet, which was in its infancy in 1996, has now spread to most corners of our planet followed closely by mobile phones, iPods and many other gadgets that we now take for granted. Is the world a happier, better place for all of this technology? This is a more debatable point yet, to be positive, I would like to think it is. The communication of ideas is paramount and the internet now allows concepts to be accessed speedily from most corners of our globe. Against this our planet is facing great challenges with global warming being considered the greatest, followed closely by the proliferation of pollutants and the ubiquitous plastic bag, which will remain in our environment for many hundreds and, in some cases, thousands of years to come.

One of the central themes of this book is that we can access a level of higher wisdom, a type of 'internet of the mind', which can provide the insights to tackle the most knotty problems. I call these higher guidance points 'quantum universities' and liken them to our physical universities with the distinction that they each one relates to a specialist area of knowledge and wisdom. With these inner tools we can draw upon a level of spiritual support and sustenance that can give insight into pursuing our lives in the most beneficial way possible. We might argue, with some justification, that the leaders of our planet, in whatever field, whether it be politics, industry, commerce or the armed services, urgently need to access this higher wisdom to ensure that their decisions are made for the highest possible good. For example, was there a better way of dealing with Saddam Hussein and the threats he posed both real and imaginary to his people and to surrounding countries?

What takes place in the macrocosm is reflected down within each of us in the ways we tackle the everyday incidents of our personal lives. In this our relationships are paramount. How do we relate to our colleagues, friends, acquaintances, adversaries, family members, our environment and above all to ourselves? I would strongly argue that despite the wonders of modern technology we still urgently need to connect with our own inner sources of wisdom and guidance to see us through the many challenges of our lives. In all the great heroic myths, the hero or heroine has to call upon some inner resource and some outside guidance, to help them overcome the obstacles that confront them in their journey. The Harry Potter books beautifully capture this theme, which is why they are so popular and touch such a deep chord in many people's hearts and minds.

This edition is a complete update on what was presented in 1996, taking into account the many changes that have taken place in our world. Its central themes, nevertheless, remain the same. Perennial wisdom is, by its definition, ageless. The challenges that faced our distant forebears through history have changed very little, for they too needed to discover techniques for accessing sources of inspiration and guidance. In their quest they devised many specific ways of achieving this objective. What is so unique in today's world is that we have extensive opportunity to explore so many wonderfully diverse approaches to spiritual enlightenment, which past cultures used for gaining insight and higher assistance. This allows us to begin to distil the collective wisdom of the ancients in a very new way. I believe this book is a step along this path.

David Furlong 2008

Introduction

A friend of mine wished to buy a particular horse for her daughter. The horse seemed ideal in all respects and appeared quite healthy. However, she used simple visualization to access her intuition, 'tuned' into the horse, and had the impression of its back legs splaying out and collapsing. An independent vet made an examination and, without any prior suggestion, said the horse was suffering from a spinal defect that would cause its legs to collapse.

Another time, an acquaintance was working with a few friends on a barn conversion. Without any warning or verbal communication between them, they all dropped their tools and fled from the building; moments later, a large timber beam crashed to the floor on the spot where they had been standing.

A number of years ago, a relative went for the first time to see a clairvoyant. After some inconsequential comments, the psychic suddenly said that she was aware of an uncle called Jim who had recently died; he wished to pass a message to her father saying that he was ok. Her father's brother Jim had indeed died two months previously and this information could not have been known to the clairvoyant.

These three cases are typical of many thousands of similar experiences that people have each year throughout the world. They powerfully suggest that information can be gathered by some unknown faculty that lies within us. Unfortunately, there is no generally accepted scientific paradigm that can explain these phenomena at present. The tendency has therefore been to dismiss any claims of paranormal or psychic activity as being either fraud or coincidence. Some researchers suggest that all psychic phenomena can be explained in terms of known psychological processes which do not involve any paranormal activity. Certainly, those who make their living as psychics may, from time to time, use such techniques to extract information from their clients. Yet the odds of the clairvoyant described above 'guessing' that a close relative called Jim had recently died must be astronomically high. How was my friend able to ascertain that the horse had a spinal problem, which showed up on a detailed veterinary examination? Something more profound than orthodox science would have us believe in must be at work here. In scientific investigations, experiments are repeated to confirm the results. Psychic function has proved extraordinarily difficult to pin down in this way. Repeated experiments have been carried out, with some success, but there are always those who will go to great lengths to explain away such findings because they contravene current scientific wisdom. It is often the case that today's impossibility becomes tomorrow's accepted norm. After all, not so long ago, scientists were claiming that the atom could not be split. In this book, I will try to offer insights from my own working experiences on how bridges can be made between science and the paranormal. Evidence is available to those who are willing to view the data through un-blinkered eyes.

It is my firm conviction that the psychic function is a natural part of us all and that, like any artistic gift, it can be developed and expressed in ways that will enhance and enrich our lives. Its applications include the development of your intuitive and creative abilities, your sensitivity and insight into situations and people, your awareness of potential future problems and how to avoid them, your ability to use healing energy to help others and so on. There are also many well documented occasions where this faculty would appear to have saved lives. One of the commanding officers in the battle of Goose Green in the Falklands war was confronted by a superior force of Argentineans, well dug in and protected, who had just repulsed his initial assault. The odds were stacked against him taking the position without considerable loss of life. In desperation that night, he just prayed for help. In an instant he knew what steps he had to take. In the morning, he sent an emissary to the Argentineans demanding their immediate surrender and against all expectations, they agreed. His action saved many lives on both sides. This is an extreme case but the principles can be readily developed and used in all aspects of your life.

Your psychic faculty has one other very important aspect. I will postulate here that there exists a global, super-intelligent level of consciousness that can be accessed through your mind. It does not matter whether you wish to call this 'God' or, as I have done here, the 'quantum psychic' realm. I believe that it was by making a connection to this level of consciousness that the officer was inspired to make the correct decision. In the past, this has also been known as the realm of the gods, which people prayed to for help and inspiration. Its function would appear to mirror very closely that of the internet today where a Google search can turn up detailed information on practically any subject. I hope to demonstrate that it was by making connections into this mental web of knowledge that many prominent scientists were able to make quantum leaps in their ideas and perceptions. Perhaps the real genius of such people as Einstein and Leonardo da Vinci was their ability to access the data contained in this other dimension. If this hypothesis is correct, there is no reason why you should not also make those connections. Indeed, the information in this book will show you how this can be done through your psychic senses.

One of the main stumbling blocks that prevent people allowing their psychic ability free expression is fear, generally because of its unknown quality. It flies in the face of all that we have been taught to believe from a rational stand-point. The encouraging news is that many pioneers have explored the way ahead of you and maps of 'the territory' are now available. Like driving a car, there can be dangers if you do not follow the Highway Code, but these are small compared with the great benefits that can result.

The word psychic also conjures up images of strange magical practices and all sorts of hocus-pocus that distort its real meaning. The root of the word psychic comes from the Greek word psyche, which refers to the soul within. So a correct definition of psychic would be 'an expression of soul consciousness'. This is another way of saying that it is a manifestation of the energy from your innermost being. Unfortunately, its pejorative associations have dominated many people's concepts and for this reason those who have scientifically studied this subject have often used the word 'psi' as a substitute. This seems to me to be an important contribution and therefore I intend to use this word, in preference to 'psychic', throughout the text.

We live in exciting times, where there are many challenges to established systems and practices. In the business world, the need for innovation and creativity is being recognized as fundamental to the long-term health and success of any company. Many innovative businesses were born and guided from the intuitive hunches of their founders. Recently, I heard that one very successful senior director never made any major decision without first consulting the I Ching (an ancient Chinese system of divination, discussed in Chapter 13). Astrologers are now advising investors in the stock market, with often better results than their more rational counterparts. I believe that as we move into an age where certainties no longer hold sway, the need for that extra insight becomes paramount.

This book is divided into four sections. Each section contains simple exercises that you can use to help the unfolding of the psi aspect of your nature. The exercises should ideally be approached in the sequence given. Some may seem more relevant than others, but all, from my experience of 35 years teaching, are important. Obviously, if you have already embarked upon your own study and training in these fields with a competent teacher, you can be selective in choosing those exercises that you feel are more appropriate for you. I would, however, like to stress the similarities with any form of artistic expression. There are certain basics that must be mastered before pressing on with the more advanced exercises. If they are neglected, problems can arise at later stages.

The first section of the book provides a model, suggesting how and why the psi function operates within us and what can be done to increase its expression. Science and traditional spiritual belief are both helpful in giving many insights into the nature of who and what we are. These ideas are presented in a logical way that I believe is useful to understanding ourselves. However it is also my intention that this should be seen as but one perspective, which does not have greater validity than some of the other models of the nature of reality that exist at present. Therefore, these concepts are not intended to be dogmatic in any sense; they are based on empirical evidence, my own experiences and, wherever possible, scientific study. Section 2 explores the expression of these forces in everyday life and lays the foundations for the inner development work of the last two sections.

Psi function can operate in two ways. It can be expressed outwardly in a directed form; healing is perhaps the most obvious example. Here the 'psi' energy flows out from you towards another person or object. Conversely, it can operate receptively, and you become the receiver of its energy. Intuition, clairvoyance, hunches and telepathy are all aspects of this mode. Section 3 will focus on all facets of the receptive mode and Section 4 will explore the outgoing or directed use of psi. The term energy should be clarified here, for science restricts the meaning of this word to the interaction of forces within the physical world which conform to known scientific laws. Psi energy does not accord with this meaning. It is not part of the electro-magnetic spectrum and does not fit into the current scientific understanding of the physical world, although some concepts in quantum mechanics, such as Heisenberg's Uncertainty Principle or Bell's Theorem, come close to giving insights into how it might operate. Yet the Oxford Dictionary also defines energy as the 'ability or capacity to produce an effect' and for want of a better expression it is in this wider context that the term energy is used in this text. In Far Eastern cultures this energy is known as Ch'i, from where we get terms such as Tai Ch'i and Ch'i Kung.

Although this book covers the basics of what you might wish to know of psi and its different modes of expression, and also includes many exercises that you can safely incorporate into your life, it should not be seen as a substitute for a good teacher. Again, taking any of the fine arts as an example, there are many Teach Yourself guides which can set you on your way and open up an enormous amount of enjoyment. Yet once you reach a certain stage of competence, having the help of someone who has working experience becomes important. A number of recommended training organizations are given in the appendix to facilitate further study.

Exploration into the nature of consciousness stands at the leading edge of scientific enquiry. Most people use but a small section of their brain power in their daily lives. The journey of the twenty-first century will almost certainly be into 'inner space' to unlock the potential that lies within us all. This is both exciting and challenging, for to be truly understood, the concepts contained in this book need to be experienced. A recipe book has little real value or its subtleties appreciated unless it is put to practical use. The techniques given in this book will work on the symbolic parts of your consciousness to unlock inner levels of awareness. They will certainly increase your insight and ability to lead a more productive, expansive life. I hope it will also give you a glimpse of the enormous power that is waiting to be tapped and of your ability to connect to this higher inner wisdom and knowledge. It is certainly a journey that has enriched my life and that of my colleagues and it is my wish that it will do the same for you.

SECTION 1

The Psychic Senses:

Mapping the Psi Territory

CHAPTER 1

The Psi Function

Most people have some level of psi experience during the course of their lives. Sometimes these experiences are so startling and inexplicable that they stand out like brilliant beacons, but in many cases they are dismissed without much thought as strange quirky coincidences. There are also those perceptions and insights which are not considered 'psi experiences' at all. Consider those times when you are thinking of someone only moments before they ring on your mobile or a text message arrives, or you bump into them on the street; or the odd intuitions or hunches that prove to be correct. There may be times when you dream about events before they happen or get a creative idea that seemed to come from nowhere; the feelings also that you get from different places. Such things can be so much part of everyday life that they are not considered unusual. Yet, as we shall see, all these fall into the broader category of 'psi experiences'.

Science has no paradigm that adequately explains why some people are able to communicate telepathically, are aware of future events, or are able to heal others over great distances. Such abilities have been well documented many times over, yet for the last 150 years the scientific establishment has been very uncomfortable with any notion of non-physical levels of consciousness and intervention into the material world. Because of the splits occurring between religion and science, it became much easier for the scientists to explore 'reality' unfettered by religious dogma; the consequence has been that generally only that which can be repeatedly tested in the laboratory crucible has been acceptable. Psi phenomena have been extraordinarily resistant to this form of repeated testing, at least until recently.

THE VALUE OF THE PSI FUNCTION

The technology in our society meets most of our physical needs and is, on the whole, very successful. Telepathic communication may be very important for so-called 'primitive' societies living close to nature with no other means of communication across large distances. Laurens Van Der Post, for example, found that the Bushmen of the Kalahari knew in advance which of several different pilots would be flying the aircraft that used their landing strip, though there was no direct radio communication. The villagers also were aware when one of their hunters had killed an eland, a very special event, and immediately set preparations for a celebration. Similar abilities have been described in detail by anthropologists in different parts of the world, particularly amongst the Aborigines and North American Indians. Yet, although many people have had the experience of thinking of someone just before they telephone, telepathy generally serves very little real purpose in today's society, where mobile phones are more handy and reliable. It is therefore valid to question the value of the psi function? Does this seemingly atrophied aspect of human consciousness really have a place in a modern world? To answer this question we need to understand what psi is all about.

In essence psi phenomena can be divided into two categories:

- Extra sensory communication and information exchange.
- Mental interaction with the physical world through non-physical means.

Parapsychologists usually refer to these two categories as ESP (extra-sensory perception) and PK (psychokinesis), but for reasons that will become apparent I prefer to use the broader definitions.

COMMUNICATION AND INFORMATION

Psi communication, channeled through your 'higher mind' or 'inner knowing', allows you to gain information not readily available through the five physical senses. This may include communicating with other individuals, but, more generally, involves accessing what Carl Jung called the 'collective unconscious'. Into this latter domain we can include the many guides, masters, and angelic beings that provide inspiration and support for us in our journey through life. In all of this we have a very interesting parallel with what is taking place at the moment at the leading edge of communication technology. The internet, a global computer information superhighway network, is now well established and available in most parts of the world. Ideas can be transmitted around the planet in an instant. With a computer you can log into this network and look up information on almost any conceivable subject. You can also send information to a particular person or company or broadcast your ideas to millions through web pages or bulletin boards. It is a facility that is available to anyone who has access to a computer and a little patience in learning how the system works.

The psi function, in its communication mode, allows us to connect into another version of this information superhighway. We might call this version a 'quantum' super-information highway. I realize that in using the term 'quantum' I may be accused of stepping on the toes of a few scientists, but it is the best term that I can think of and one that has already been used by people like Dr Deepak Chopra in his book *Quantum Healing* to describe a higher dimensional reality that stands behind the physical world.

This 'quantum' information highway has many similar functions to the internet with some important advantages and a few disadvantages.

Imagine for a moment an interconnecting web that exists on a mental level, with the potential to link everyone together - a system that can be easily accessed through your mind. Imagine also that databases containing information on all the individuals that have ever lived on this planet are linked in to it. This highway also has a special facility that allows you to look forward into the potential future, by analyzing, on a collective, as well as, an individual basis, everybody's thoughts and intentions. It is also able to look backwards into the past thereby enabling you to determine the consequences of any of your actions. Imagine a highway unfettered by the strictures of time or space that can access the collective knowledge of the finest minds that have ever lived upon this planet so that the highest levels of wisdom are available to you. Is such an idea a fanciful notion?

In this book, I intend to present solid information to support this exciting concept and show you how you can start to access this 'quantum' network. It is a system that is open to all and many people use its facilities unconsciously. Creative and innovative people need constant access to new ideas. Where do these ideas come from? Is it just neurons firing off in the brain, or are there people who have a knack of plugging into this other level of information and are constantly fed by another realm of consciousness? It is proposed here that your psi function, your intuitive faculty, is no more than an inner computer terminal which will allow you to access information from this other dimensional reality.

I wonder if you have ever been confronted by a major problem which seemed unsolvable and then something inside you clicked and you just 'knew' the answer with great certainty. I believe that the answer to any problem can become more conscious or readily available to you when you learn some simple techniques.

It is these intuitive flashes that have often inspired great scientists like Einstein with new insights that have taken knowledge forward into a new dimension. The German scientist Professor Friedrich Kekule admitted that the discovery of the molecular ring structure of benzene came to him in a dream where he saw a snake swallowing its tail. He awoke realizing that this was a symbolic answer to his problem.

Although important scientific discoveries come from a few individuals, everyone has areas of their life where foreknowledge, insight, and information are important. Whatever your occupation, there are times when decisions need to be made. Making the right decision helps us to avoid some of life's pitfalls.

But what are the disadvantages of the quantum information highway? The major disadvantage involves the time required to learn how you can access this level of awareness and the potential for one's wires to become crossed so that incorrect information comes through. The various exercises, safeguards and checks given in this book will help to avoid this difficulty.

Information overload The other main problem involves situations where an individual's 'inner computer' is locked into this quantum level and they are not able to process all the information coming through. They can feel swamped by ideas and energies that are overwhelming and, because they have not learned how to turn off their computer, they feel no respite. Some people who read this book will already be beginning to experience this type of phenomenon, without really appreciating what is happening to them. This is naturally quite disturbing and sometimes causes people to seek psychiatric help. We access this network through our minds and anyone who practices meditation techniques will have already started this process. It can also be sparked off by drug use, but this is not recommended as it is likely to distort the messages.

Understanding what is happening is one of the most beneficial ways of relieving this problem. It is then possible to integrate and balance this aspect within the rest of one's life. Another common problem is when individuals start to become consciously aware of disharmonious energies from other people or places, which is then felt to cause disruption to themselves.

There will always be energies that are harmonious to you and ones that are not. You will need to learn how to protect yourself from those psi energies that can cause problems. I am not suggesting that such energies are bad or evil, only that the quality of some energies might disrupt your equilibrium. In the same way, if you were to go and sunbathe without adequate protection you would end up getting burnt. This book contains simple exercises which will show you how to protect yourself naturally from such influences. All this comes under the heading of a psi 'highway code', mentioned in the introduction.

INTERACTING OR POSITIVE PSI

This form of psi is usually referred to as psychokinesis: an individual brings about changes in the physical world through some as yet unknown mechanism. Uri Geller's spoon-bending ability is an example of psychokinesis. Another example has been demonstrated in some fascinating research led by Professor Jahn at Princeton University, where many individuals were able to influence electrical circuits or random generators using their minds *(Margins of Reality: The Role of Consciousness in the Physical World,* Jahn, R. and Dune, B., Harcourt Brace Jovanovich, 1987). Like telepathy, these abilities appear, as yet, to have little practical relevance to the world in which we live, however, what is usually overlooked is that the most common way that this aspect of the mind works is by influencing another mind at a subconscious level. This manifests in family dynamics and interpersonal relationships, where unspoken wishes and beliefs have a powerful impact on the individuals holding them.

One of its most practical expressions is through healing. In these cases, it is claimed that an energy is broadcast which can help another person speed up their healing processes or, in some cases, reverse a potentially fatal illness. In a famous experiment by Dr Randolph Byrd, he used a double-blind test to assess the effectiveness of prayer/healing for heart patients at his hospital in San Francisco *(Healing Words.* Dossey, L., HarperCollins, 1993). From a list of over 400 patients who had been admitted with coronary problems, two hundred names were passed on to a number of prayer groups in his area. No-one in the hospital knew of the experiment, except for a few senior staff, so there could be no collusion between doctors and patients. Moreover, only the first names of the patients were passed to the healers, who were asked to pray regularly for the names on the list. The results were so stunning and so beneficial, that one commentator suggested that had a drug company come up with these results, it would have been hailed as a new wonder drug.

This experiment demonstrates the two sides of this amazing quantum information highway. Firstly, in its positive projection through healing, individuals benefited. Secondly, the prayer 'found' the person to whom it was directed through their first names and some brief information about their particular case only. Just sending a thought to locate a particular individual allowed the 'quantum directory' to find the person. Empirical evidence from healers all over the world backs up this idea. It would seem that if your intention is to connect mentally to a particular person, even if you know only their first name, then you will do so.

In this book, you will learn ways to use your mind to influence your life path. There are many books on positive thinking, which is really an aspect of this outgoing psi function. I believe that if you project a positive image of what you wish to achieve, a dynamic energy will carry you to your goal.

YOUR PSI ABILITIES

So, psi has two distinct functions. One allows you to access a super-intelligent level of consciousness, which I have allied with Jung's 'collective unconscious' and called a 'quantum information highway'. The other can be used to influence events in your life in a positive and creative way. One of the most practical and demonstrable outlets in this form is healing.

Forty years ago, the idea of the internet would have been perceived as a pipedream. Now it is a reality. The idea of a quantum information super highway on a mental level might also seem a fanciful idea. Yet if the information that I have accessed about the future (using this quantum highway) is correct, in the not too distant future it will be a commonplace concept, with individuals learning many different techniques to make their own connections.

As we stand at the beginning of the twenty-first century, new perspectives have started to open the door to the possibilities displayed by many psi practitioners. Evidence is now available that shows the remarkable abilities that lie within human consciousness. The quantum mind concept is no longer a fanciful notion but is something that can be practically aspired to. All it requires is an ability to tap into this global consciousness network that contains a wisdom that can transcend the limitations of the perceived physical world. The ability to access this level of inner knowing can have far-reaching consequences for the success and fulfillment of your life. Ultimately this can also feed into helping humanity make the necessary changes in our collective lifestyles so that we can live in harmony with the planet and break out of this present potentially self-destructive cycle. This book will show you how you can start this process.

CHAPTER 2

Psi Energy

Science tells us in Einstein's famous theorem that energy and matter are interchangeable ($e = mc^2$). The whole of the cosmos is held together by energy, but to understand more fully the psi function we need to consider levels of energy beyond the physical realm. Your physical body has its levels of energy, but so also does your emotional self, mind and spiritual self. We might imagine this as different bands of energy continually exchanging information. The physical bands of energy are locked in time and space, whilst the spiritual realms are unfettered by the space/time continuum. In his book, *Clairvoyant Reality*, Dr Lawrence LeShan called this the clairvoyant realm. He postulated that from this realm the higher consciousness aspect of you can connect across time and space as though they were no barrier. By simply thinking of someone, you create a link between you that can allow energy to flow; the stronger the thought, the greater the likelihood of this communication being received by the conscious mind. This is why people will often pick up in advance the telephone call that is about to be made.

BROADCASTING AND RECEIVING ENERGY

The first concept to put across is the idea that you are both broadcasting and receiving 'energy' across a frequency band that includes the thoughts and emotions of others. Research by Professor Rhine into telepathy showed that some people were better senders and some better receivers of this energy; the reasons for this will be explained later in this book. Some individuals easily pick up the energies, thoughts or feelings of those around them. This is a natural expression of the psi function. Others are better broadcasters of this energy, which can be used for healing or simply stimulating and enthusing others. Winston Churchill was adept at directing this form of energy through his words, which motivated and inspired many people. The power that he exerted came from the potency of his conviction. The same words spoken by someone who did not truly believe in the message being delivered would have had nothing like the same inspirational quality.

If you think about incidents in your own life in the light of this idea, you will often remember moments when you have been influenced or have influenced other individuals in this way. This can usually happen at quite a subtle level. There are occasions when people go into a room after an argument and are immediately aware of a tension. This is often put down to non-verbal clues that individuals are displaying, but I believe that there is always a subtle energy residue that can affect us. Such energies are often more discernible within buildings. Think of some places that felt very uplifting and beneficial and some that were disturbing. This intangible energy leaves its mark on a place and others can then be affected by it.

RESONANCE

The way that psi energy is transmitted between individuals is through resonance. At a simple level, when a tuning fork, pitched to the same note as another one close by, is sounded, then the other will start to vibrate. Energy is being transmitted between them. Professor Allan Wolf stated in an article:

> The fundamental proposition is that everything is vibrating, everything is vibration. If you can vibrate with it, or attune to whatever is vibrating, then resonance is created; then you have a way of transferring energy back and forth. (*Leading Edge* magazine, Winter 1992, issue 6.)

By thinking a particular thought, a resonance is set up in your mind which is broadcast both to your body and out to whoever is listening on your frequency. Similarly, you will also pick up information that is operating on your frequency levels, which is generated by others. Because of their genetic similarities identical twins will often display powerful psychic connections and be fully aware of this subtle level of communication between them.

PSI AWARENESS

There are a number of factors that determine how much you experience through your receptive psi faculty. Your normal thinking process will block much incoming data, unless you have deliberately programmed yourself to be sensitive to it. The day-to-day events of a normal life take up most of our attention. It is only when something becomes extreme or we are in a very quiet receptive mood that this subtle level breaks through. There are many people today using meditation as a means of accessing their inner self and providing moments of tranquility in their life. These disciplines will all help this other-dimensional connection.

Some people are naturally very sensitive and aware. In the extreme, their receiving station is tuned to picking up minute signals and they can become overwhelmed by amplified discordant sound. Such people will sometimes require help shutting down or re-balancing the incoming signals because they find them so overwhelming. A simple test is to ask yourself how easily you cope in a crowded situation such as a supermarket. Do you find yourself being agitated by other people's presence? If so you almost certainly are picking up too much of their psi energy.

Attitudes also play an important part, which is one of the reasons why science has not been too successful with its experiments into psi phenomena. If a scientist firmly believes something is not possible, the strength of that thought will impede the receptivity of the psychic carrying out the experiment. To avoid this, most experiments nowadays try to use a double-blind test procedure to ensure a less biased response. If you firmly believe that psi abilities are impossible, you will immediately block their effects; conversely, the more that you can accept the possibility, the more that it will become a reality in your life.

RESONANCE ACROSS OCTAVES

There is an additional idea that can be added to the concept of resonance. In music theory energy can be exchanged between two notes pitched at a similar frequency. This energy can also be transmitted across octaves. In other words if you played middle C on a piano, then every other C note would start to vibrate. This idea is important because esoteric schools and belief systems suggest that there are many levels of energy or vibration beyond the physical. Within us, we could say that one level relates to our physical bodies, one to the emotions, one to the mind and yet another to the spirit, soul or life essence. In this theory, if you think a thought, 'resonance' transmits its message to both the emotions and the body. This concept provides a simple explanation for the psychosomatic causes of illness. Similarly, substances like alcohol, taken into the body, will affect us on an emotional, mental and spiritual level. There is a continual two-way communication taking place within us all the time.

If you wish to test out this idea for yourself, think of the last time that you felt any fear or strong emotion and decide where you experienced it within your body. Was it in the pit of your stomach, in your chest area, in your throat or perhaps in your head? Now ask your friends or acquaintances the same question and you will see that they would have experienced the physical sensation of different emotions in different parts of their bodies.

ENERGY DEPLETION

We require energy for all activities and we process it in many ways. On a psi level, energy is normally recharged at night and expended during the day. This is one of the non-physical reasons why sleep is necessary. Energy discharges are normally accelerated when we come into contact with other people, in a similar way that the battery of a radio runs down when it is being used. Therefore those individuals who come in contact with large numbers of demanding people are likely to feel this draining effect most acutely.

The draining effect of this depletion can sometimes be very marked. You have probably found yourself sitting with someone, perhaps an elderly relative, and quite suddenly feeling totally exhausted. This is sometimes put down to a drop in sugar levels within the body, but the psi explanation is that a discharge of energy takes place between you. Energy always seeks equilibrium. Imagine two reservoirs of water, one full and one nearly empty, which are on the same level. As soon as there is a connection between the two, the water will drain from the full tank into the empty one, until both are half-full. The psi explanation is that an analogous process occurs when you connect with others whose energy is depleted. Some individuals who find it difficult to recharge themselves during sleep will act as leeches on the energies of others in an unconscious way.

Details on how you can avoid these problems will be given in the chapter on healing.

THE WISDOM OF THE SELF

Some individuals, either through training or natural ability, are skilled in accessing information from the quantum realm. When you wish to get information through the internet, you need to give your computer the correct instructional codes, which are then sent as a series of vibrational pulses through the telephone line to the correct terminal. In the same way, how you program your mind will determine what you get back from the mental 'quantum' realm.

Most people access this dimension unconsciously. There are a few who have latched on to its potential and are starting to explore its dimensions through different meditation techniques. In the past, those who have done so with any clarity, such as Leonardo da Vinci, would have been regarded as geniuses. By consciously knowing what 'codes' to transmit, you can open up a vast range of information that can help in all areas of your life. One of the most important aspects of religious belief is giving adherents access to some of these codes. By offering up prayers to a particular deity, information can be exchanged and help given. For many, this remains one of the most important ways of connecting into these other realms of reality. However, although a moral perception is important when broadcasting energy to others, it is not necessary to be religious in the accepted sense to access this 'quantum' informational realm. Your inner self can act as a beacon, calling for help for whatever problem confronts you. As in all walks of life, there are pitfalls to be avoided, which will be covered in this book.

Many people are daunted when they first start to use computers. Similarly, there are those who are frightened by the thought of accessing realms of information which are not found through the written or spoken word. With a bit of perseverance and courage, you will find that it is no more difficult than using the computer as a tool to gain knowledge on whatever you seek. There are many levels of consciousness available to help you on your journey through life. With some of the present levels of uncertainty in the areas of work, finance and health, giving yourself the opportunity to access this quantum realm will give you an edge in all your decision-making. It will not necessarily stop you making all mistakes, but I believe it will greatly reduce them. Remember, this 'quantum' mental realm can access the potential futures that are open to you: the effect on your life if you make decision a) as opposed to decision b). How often have you made a decision and wished that you could have seen the outcome before you acted?

THE LEVELS OF CONSCIOUSNESS

Inscribed over the doorway of the temple of Apollo in Delphi, Greece, is the statement, 'Man know thyself'. The quest for understanding who and what we are often begins when we stand in front of a mirror and ask, 'Who am I?' This was certainly the case for me. We exist on a physical level, experiencing emotions and thoughts, but what is the 'I' that experiences and is there any real purpose behind our existence?

One of the most fascinating facets of human experience to come to the fore in recent years is the research into what has been called a 'near-death experience' or NDE. These events generally occur when a person is at the edge of clinical death. In the first stage, the consciousness of the person is felt to leave the body and view what is taking place from another perspective. In the video *Visions of Hope,* researcher Dr Elisabeth Kübler-Ross stated that to check the evidence for this perception, she sought out blind people who had had a NDE. She asked them to describe what they had 'seen', which she then attempted to verify by questioning the people who were present at the time. In all cases their descriptions proved to be remarkably accurate and this, as we know, is a medical impossibility for blind people cannot see. She was forced to conclude that the only satisfactory explanation was the one that the patients themselves gave: that some aspect of their consciousness had separated itself from their bodies which enabled them to perceive clearly what was taking place.

In his book *The Truth in the Light,* leading British neuro-psychiatrist Dr Peter Fenwick describes over three hundred and fifty cases of people who had a near-death experience, which could not be explained in simple medical terms. These strongly suggest that some aspect of consciousness is able to separate itself from the body, giving a foretaste of the afterlife. A similar study by Dutch researcher Dr Willem van

Lommel, a cardiologist at the Rynstate Hospital in Arnhem, included the case of a man brought into the Nijmegen hospital after a heart attack. He states:

> "He arrived 45 minutes after having a cardiac arrest in such bad shape - no breathing, no circulation and deeply unconscious - that he was given little chance of survival. He was put on a respirator, which meant that the nurse had to remove his dentures. When he came round a week later, he recognized that nurse, who had been with him only when he was deeply unconscious, when she happened to walk into the unit. He immediately said, 'Good to see you. You put my dental plate on the tray with the other instruments, so could you get it back for me, please?' "

Dr van Lommel claims that his study proves that near-death experiences are not caused by drugs, medication, and shortage of oxygen, the release of endorphins (the brain's pain killers) or any other physical factor. His conclusion is simple:

> "As a scientist I can't prove that there is life after death, but I am convinced that there is something in our being, call it consciousness or the Self or the divine part of ourselves, which will not die, though our bodies may."

In the second stage of the NDE, the person will sense that they are traveling along a tunnel towards a light. When they emerge, they sometimes meet individuals or relatives that have died and will often later describe an extraordinary feeling of peace and well-being. They are then told that now is not their time to pass over and they find themselves being drawn back into their bodies.

The most significant aspect of this experience is the complete freedom from any fear of death; instead, people look forward to the moment when they cross over into the afterlife. There is often also a significant change in their outlook and perspective on life, with material accomplishments becoming less important than human relationships.

The near-death experience provides powerful evidence that part of your consciousness survives the death of the physical body and continues to exist in another realm. We can speculate on what that might be like, but the important point to believe at this stage is that part of your consciousness can detach itself from the body and has access to other realms of reality.

This concept is taken a stage further in a remarkable book by Dr Michael Newton entitled *Journey of Souls*. This is based on the collective regressed experiences of hundreds of his patients who described they recalled in the space between a series of lives on the Earth that is after they have died and passed out of one life and before they returned to another physical body. When I first read Newton's work I was excited because it tallied with my own inner journeying and affirmed much of what I had already experienced.

Some of the concepts that Newton presents are that we make a freewill conscious choice to incarnate into the physical world choosing our parents and a life pattern that has already been broadly pre-determined. When we incarnate part of our 'higher' consciousness remains in the soul or spirit realm and has access to many levels of support, help and guidance. Souls will also work together in small self-supporting groups and often these groups will incarnate at the same time with the individuals meeting up at different stages of a lifetime. You might like to reflect on the people in your life who might be part of your soul group.

Finally when we choose a challenging life this might be for spiritual reasons and have nothing to do with bad karma (see Glossary). For example, if I truly wished to learn 'forgiveness' there would be little point in me incarnating into a family of warm loving people or associating with colleagues that were always encouraging. As a general rule, when confronting a challenging or distressing situation, it is always a good habit to ask yourself, "Why have I chosen to put myself through this experience?" Your 'higher' mind always knows the answer if you are sufficiently open to receiving the information that is available.

THE POLARITY OF THE SELF

In the light of the above ideas, we can say your being is a spectrum: at one end is the physical body, with which we are all familiar; at the other is the inner consciousness, soul or spiritual self, or whatever term you care to choose. Every other aspect of you - your mind, subconscious and emotions - falls between these two poles. Many schools of thought suggest that there is a stepping-down in energy between these distinct layers of the self, which we can liken to the different octaves on the piano. The highest or finest energy layer of your being is your spiritual self, while the meanest or densest is your physical body. Your emotional energies are closer in frequency to your physical body, while your thoughts and mind are closer to your soul, according to these traditions.

When psi energy is exchanged between people it will reflect the level that it has been generated from. Therefore, an emotional discharge from another person will hit us first at an emotional level before being reflected to our thoughts and bodies. Expression of powerful beliefs or conviction will often sway the mind of a listener, even against their better judgment. Sales techniques use methods based on similar ideas - although in many cases this mental manipulation is carried out without fully realizing what is happening at an energy level.

SEXUAL ENERGY

Another area where we experience subtle energy exchange is through sexual encounters. There are some individuals who exude sexual energy to such a high degree that you just have to be in their company to be 'turned on'. This has nothing to do with good looks, but is linked to the energies stored in the sexual center which is one of the chakric centers (see Glossary). Specific sexual practices have been used by many people and cultures to bring forward or create different states of awareness or consciousness. Sexual energy can be channeled and used very creatively, in many different areas of your life, if you know how to focus this force.

This does not mean that we need many sexual encounters for this energy to flow properly, for apart from its procreative element it can be channeled into any creative project such as a piece of music or work of art. There are valid reasons, in psi energy terms, why many monastic institutions practice celibacy. However, this does not mean you have to be celibate to be spiritual. On the contrary expressing the functions of being human in a natural way can allow us to more fully integrate our divine nature. It is how you use sexual energy that is important.

SYNCHRONICITY

There is a scientific principle that when two similar energies meet, a pulse is set up that will immediately bring them into alignment. This process is called 'entrainment'. It was first observed by a Dutch scientist called Christian Huyens in 1665 when he observed the pendulums of two wall clocks swinging in precise time together. When he separated the clocks, the pendulums moved out of phase, but returned again to synchronicity as soon as they were brought together. This principle, occurs whenever two or more oscillators are pulsating at nearly the same rate. They will tend to lock together to beat at exactly the same time. It has been noted that women living together will often start to menstruate at the same time. We can think of this as if an energy frequency has been set up, creating a pulse that leads to synchronization of their periods.

This concept has important consequences for our well-being. Within us, it is well recognized that health depends upon our body, emotions, mind and spirit being in harmony. If any part of our being is 'at odds' with the rest, for example during emotional trauma, distortions will be set up that can affect our health. Using the piano metaphor, to achieve good health the piano must be 'in tune' so that energy can flow across the whole of the keyboard. When our energy connects with that of another, oscillations are set up and this will tend to draw the two sets of energies into synchronization. In other words, part of us will get pulled slightly 'out of tune'. This can have the effect of disrupting our internal equilibrium. This is why sensitive people can sometimes feel battered by the disruptive energies of others. Fortunately, there is much that you can do to prevent this problem getting out of hand. This will be fully covered in the next chapter.

YIN AND YANG

Polarities run through all aspects of life. For example, all computer technology is based on electrical pulses that are either on or off. All of the amazing things that are generated through or by this technology are derived from this very simple switching. There is a tendency to see polarities only in their extreme form. Something is right or wrong, on or off, good or bad, positive or negative and so on. In the East, this extreme view was regarded as being inherently unstable. Much rather, said the Chinese sages, to perceive energy, known as Ch'i, weaving continually back and forth between two polarity extremes, which they called Yang and Yin. Yang is the outgoing, masculine, positive pole, and Yin is the receptive, feminine, negative pole. The Yang/Yin symbol (see page 135) expressed this idea and also contained the notion that within extreme Yang existed Yin and vice versa. These ideas are discussed in more detail in Chapter 13.

The Chinese philosophy espoused the idea that energy rarely reached an extreme position, but more generally flowed between these two poles; things were rarely white or black but generally a shade of grey. A similar concept has found its way into technology based upon what is called 'fuzzy logic'. A fuzzy logical system tries to evaluate the real needs of a situation and adjusts itself accordingly. For example, one fuzzy logic patent describes a dishwasher that assesses the number of dishes and the amount of food encrusted on the plates and adjusts its wash cycles accordingly.

Psi energy performs a dance within us, moving between the poles of Yang and Yin, so that we are transmitting and receiving energy synchronistically, balancing and re-balancing our inner flows all the time. The notes of our inner pianos are not fixed rigidly but move in response to the signals coming through to us. To maintain balance and inner harmony, there needs to be continual adjustment. Fortunately, this happens without too much conscious thought on our behalf. However, as you start to become more aware of the psi facet of your life, to become more receptive to the subtle messages that come through from these other realms, you will need also to be more aware of consciously balancing your energies.

FLAVORS OF ENERGY

In Yang and Yin terms, we could say that psi energy has two 'flavors'. One is outgoing and expansive and the other is passive and receptive, in practice psi energy has many more flavors than this. In this book, we will look at how you can begin to appreciate and use different qualities of energy for specific tasks. For example, the quality of the energy that you would need to start a new project or business would be very different from that required for a space for meditation or prayer. One situation demands a dynamic, clear, direct energy, and the other favors something that is calming, gentle and introspective.

Peoples in the past understood these arrays of energy and used the symbolism of their gods and goddesses to provide keys or links into what was required for any situation. This was done by invoking, calling upon or supplicating the god or goddess that was deemed relevant. How you can link into these different nuances of energy will be covered more fully in later chapters.

SELF-AWARENESS EXERCISES

Before concluding this chapter there are three self-awareness and re-energizing exercises that you might want to practice. These will be the foundation for other exercises in later chapters and will start the process of inner development. These exercises have been adapted from my book, *The Healer Within.*

If at any moment your mind starts to wander, go back to the beginning of the exercise. This is an important self-discipline which will start to train your mind in concentrated thinking. If, for example, you reach your knees and then start to think about someone's knee problems, take your thoughts back to your toes and start again. By this process you will be disciplining your mind, which has sometimes been seen as a monkey, leaping from idea to idea. We need to tame this monkey gently, so that it comes under our control. It does not matter in this case that you do not reach the brow, for it is the discipline that is important. Nor does it matter how quickly or slowly you can carry out this exercise. Meditation takes practice and unfortunately there are no short cuts.

BASIC BODY AWARENESS EXERCISE (time: 3 to 5 mins)

Aim: To provide body awareness for general Ch'i balancing

You will need to find a place and time where you can be undisturbed. Adopt one of the following postures:

- Sit in an upright chair with a straight back, feet uncrossed and resting on the floor and hands palms down on your thighs.

- Kneel, using a meditation stool, and again link your thumb and index finger.

- It is important to keep the back straight and not slump down.

BASIC BODY AWARENESS EXERCISE (continued)
Note: Different hand positions known as Mudras reflect different aims in meditation. Linking the thumb with the first finger symbolically connects the spiritual self with 'ego' consciousness.

- Direct your attention to your toes. Try to be fully aware of each toe in turn. If you can imagine it, try to sense how your toes would view the rest of you. This suggests that our toes are conscious, which you may discover when you can carry out the exercise. Feel that all the energy around your toes is balanced and flowing in a harmonious way

- Slowly move your consciousness from your toes to your feet, carrying out the same process, and then on up your body, focusing on each part in turn.

- When you reach your eyes, pause and then focus on a spot between and slightly above your eyes. This is known as the 'Third Eye' centre. In yogic philosophy, this is one of the major control centers of the body and can be used for balancing your energies. Imagine, if you can, that your whole consciousness is centered on this spot, and then sense that all the energies within you are balanced and harmonious. Hold this thought for a few moments, before bringing yourself bringing yourself back to full waking consciousness.

CONNECTING TO YOUR INNER WISDOM

In the next exercise there is sometimes a tendency to seek your inner wisdom, which can be symbolized as an 'inner-light' outside yourself, i.e. in some space above one's head. The challenge of being in a physical body is to ground and earth the spiritual aspect within you so that you fully experience physical reality while you are still in touch with your spiritual self. The first step in this process is awakening to the spiritual within, but this can sometimes result in a desire to detach from the physical. In energetic terms, if you project your consciousness away from your body there is a danger that some aspect of your psyche will split off.

The effect of this will mean that it becomes difficult to balance your energies within the physical. This is why meditating for a long period of time is often not desirable, as in this case the meditation can become a form of 'cop-out' from normal living. Therefore try not to project yourself into any light or spiritual space that is outside you. Rather, make sure that the light is firmly located within your physical body, before connecting with it. This grounding process is an important part of all inner development work.

If the following exercise is practiced regularly it will become possible to immediately connect to your higher levels of wisdom and guidance.

CONNECTING TO YOUR INNER LIGHT EXERCISE
(time: 3 to 5 mins)

Aim: **The inner light is a reflection of your spiritual self. This is one of the easiest ways to connect to your inner source.**

- Sit in one of the postures described in the last exercise and close your eyes.
- Carry out the body awareness exercise. With practice, this can be shortened to a quick check to make sure that you are fully relaxed.
- When you have spent a few moments balancing the energies of your 'Third Eye' or 'Brow Centre', think of your inner spiritual self and try to sense, visualize, or feel this as a tiny flame of light within your body.
- When you have located the flame slowly move your consciousness into the light, so that you become the light and it becomes you. What do you experience?
- Hold that thought for a few moments before withdrawing, and then slowly bringing yourself back to full waking reality.

Note: if you fear fire (flame of light) you could use another symbol for your spiritual self. A golden chalice would be a good alternative.

The above exercise is a simple way of starting the process of connecting to your inner wisdom or spiritual self. Like the body awareness exercise, it does not need to take a long time, but starts the process of opening up your inner lines of communication.

When you feel you have mastered these techniques there are a number of important supplementary exercises that you can try.

Repeating these exercises will benefit you on many levels. In my forty years experience of working with many thousands of clients they have confirmed how helpful they have been. I have come to realize that at quite a deep level many people do not really want to be here on this planet because of the need to confront some difficult and challenging situations that life presents. If you can recognize the difference in energetic quality between doing those things that you really enjoy doing and those that you do not you may get a sense of this yourself. It raises the importance of learning to embrace life to the full. When you do this wholehearted all of your experiences take on a very different quality.

The final exercise in the section will help you balance some of the different facets of your being.

ENERGY BALANCING EXERCISE (time: 3 to 5 mins)

Aim: To balance the energies of your being

You will need first to imagine a pair of scales. On these scales you will be able to place whatever you like about yourself to see whether it is in balance. For example, you could symbolically place your physical self on one side and your spiritual self on the other. If the scales balance you will immediately know that you have a good balance between these two aspects of your being. If it tips to the physical you will need to work on bringing the spiritual side of your life more to the fore. If the scales are weighted on the side of the spiritual you will need to work on coming to grips with the physical world. The most important aim is balance.

If you are not comparing two differing aspects, as in the above example, yet simply want to know whether a situation is balanced or not, then place the symbol of a white feather on one side of the scales and the situation or part of yourself on the other. It does not matter which side you choose.

- Sit in one of the postures mentioned previously and close your eyes.
- Carry out the body awareness exercise. With practice, this can be shortened to 1 to 2 minutes.
- Connect to your inner light and then imagine the Sun or a star is right above your head and you are drawing a beam of sunlight (starlight) down through the top of your head and linking it to your inner light. What do you experience?
- Next imagine that you have in front of you a pair of scales, placing on them the parts that need to be balanced.
- Check whether the scales are evenly poised. If not, ask yourself what you need to add or take away from each side to bring the scales into balance. You might sense that you need to add light or love to one side or another, or remove some unwanted energy.
- If you need help to get the scales in balance then call upon the energy of the Sun to assist you. You can imagine that you are filling the scales with light.
- When the scales balance, bring yourself back to full conscious reality.

Note: For some people it may take quite a time to get the scales to balance. Indeed, if your energies are seriously out of balance you may have to repeat this exercise on a number of occasions. Keep persevering if at first you do not succeed.

Although this exercise is carried out at a mental level the effect will translate itself down through every part of your being. It may bring some situation to the surface that you may have been avoiding so you will need to persevere.

All balancing exercises of this nature will help maintain your health and vitality. These exercises should all be carried out on a regular basis. I normally incorporate them into a single meditation procedure that I adopt most days. As I have said, it need not take a long time - five to ten minutes per day is sufficient. In my experience, the beneficial effects will be well worth the effort.

CHAPTER 3

Psi Protection

One of the most problematic areas of psi development is the consequential increase in sensitivity to all energies. It is rather like turning up the volume on your radio so that you can pick up a very distant signal. This is fine while you listen to that program, but if you move the tuning dial without first turning down the volume, you might suddenly 'tune into' a station that is very close, which then blasts you with the noise. In a similar way, there are many people today who are metaphorically developing the sensitivity of their inner receivers, who then find being in everyday situations very disturbing. This can become very distressing if the necessary 'de-tuning' precautions have not also been taken. If you know the precautionary procedures you can avoid most of these problems.

According to the psi system of thought, energy is flowing within us and through us all the time. This is a natural process. As I said in the last chapter, there is a subtle balance between the energy of your spiritual self and that of your body, which I likened to the link between the various octaves on the piano. For energy to be exchanged between individuals, we can imagine that the fine tuning on their pianos needs to be adjusted. This is what lovers unconsciously do, but in practice it occurs whenever we set up a sympathetic link with another person. Another way to understand this process is to imagine that you are a two-way radio broadcasting a particular signal on a frequency of say 240 MHz (megahertz). You meet someone whose radio is tuned to receive a signal on 242 MHz. At first their reception of your signals is distorted but through internal adjustment you both re-tune to 241 MHz so that clear energy exchange can take place between you. Remember this is not physical energy, but something that exists on a subtle level. Your emotions are broadcasting energies; your thoughts are broadcasting energies, as is also your spiritual self. We each maintain our own level of inner balance so that in the above example when these two individuals have separated they will need to readjust their sets back to 240 MHz and 242 MHz respectively. This process normally takes place unconsciously, but if a person becomes stuck for any reason a distortion is created in their internal energy balance. This is where the piano analogy is most appropriate.

Let us suppose that two people meet on an emotional level and their note frequency corresponds metaphorically with 'A' on the piano. For maximum psi energy to be exchanged, those two notes need to be pitched at exactly the same frequency. These two notes will normally be slightly off-pitch so an internal adjustment will have to be made to bring them into harmony. This, in turn, will throw their other internal frequencies slightly 'out of tune'. When they disconnect, both individuals will then have to spend time re-balancing their energy fields. This re-balancing process is generally unconscious and is one of the normal functions of sleep. However, the more finely tuned the instrument, the more necessary the internal adjustments, particularly for those individuals working with psychologically or emotionally disturbed people. This is where meditation and re-balancing exercises become very important.

THE AURA

Problems arise when your inner energies get distorted by incoming influences from another person. In the psi system, it is generally perceived that we all have a natural defense mechanism that helps us deal with this predicament. Traditionally this has been called the aura, which acts in an analogous way to the Earth's atmosphere. Our planet's protective shield cuts out some of the harmful radiation from the Sun and burns up meteorites before they do too much damage to the surface. The task of your aura is to protect you from incoming energies that could potentially upset your equilibrium.

The aura is traditionally perceived by clairvoyants as an energy field that emanates from the physical body for a distance of a few feet and contains different colors, reflecting the health and state of consciousness of the person in question.

At a physical level, protection is such a natural part of our lives that we rarely give it much thought unless something goes wrong. For example, although the skin provides one level of protection, it is not sufficient to compensate for fluctuations in temperature, so we wear clothes. Our immune system maintains health and our homes provide an ambient climate in which to live.

In all of these cases, giving additional conscious support to our basic systems increases their effectiveness. We wear different types of clothes according to what we are likely to be exposed to. We heat and insulate our homes to make them more comfortable and we have vaccinations or take antibiotics to assist our immune system. In a similar way, in the psi system your aura can be strengthened and its effectiveness increased so that you are not so easily upset by disturbed energies.

Another way of looking at this consequence of psi development is to imagine that you are in a room with no doors and windows, so that you can only hear faint sounds coming in from outside. To improve your perception of what is happening 'outside' you knock some holes in the walls and immediately you discover some amazing sights and sounds. If this is a house, getting a view of a street or open countryside for the first time would be a wonderful new experience, as long as the Sun was shining and there were not any discordant sounds. But imagine what it would be like if it started to hail, or the council workmen came to dig up the road? These openings would then be the cause of considerable inner disturbance. The solution, of course, is to put in doors, windows and curtains so that you can adjust your response to outside influences to a level that is comfortable for you. The same process applies to your aura which, in practice, is no more difficult to adjust than selecting the clothes you will wear for any particular occasion.

METHODS OF PROTECTION

The range of different methods of psi protection is enormous. You can use many different types of psi protection depending upon what you are likely to encounter, as you can wear different types of protective clothing depending on the weather, but in most instances, protection can be kept at a very simple level and will be very effective.

Some people get worried that, in protecting themselves, they will be cutting off their natural sensitivity. This will not happen, unless you choose it to. Your psi protection will adjust itself naturally to balance incoming signals so that you will still be able to 'pick up' what is important, but will not be overwhelmed by an influx of any disturbing energy.

Another problem involves people who regard protection as a frightened response against what is feared. Some people argue that using protection in this way actually encourages the fear to manifest itself. I do not agree with this sentiment, for firstly fear does have its place in preserving us from dangerous situations.

Secondly, we do not wear clothes in fear of the weather, but through a desire to be comfortable when we face inclement temperatures.

All psi energy at this level is controlled through your mind. Additionally, some physical objects, such as a Christian cross or the 'Hand of Fatima', have acquired reputations for acting as protective symbols. Because of how they have been linked through people's beliefs, they may also help. Developing psi protection through your thoughts is, however, the most effective method and a couple of exercises are included in this chapter.

Ideally, a protection exercise should be carried out before any psi work is undertaken. It can also become a very useful addition before and after meditation exercises. I always spend a few moments each day, when I get up and just before going to bed, in balancing and protecting my aura.

With practice, and by reducing the time spent relaxing, it can become an almost instantaneous response that can be called upon in any emergency situation. Practice is important. You can soon learn to carry out this exercise with your eyes open. Try doing it when you have a few moments to yourself, on the train to work, or during a coffee break. The more that you do this, the stronger your auric protection becomes for, in my experience, each attempt has a cumulative effect.

PROTECTION EXERCISE (time: 10 mins)

Aim: To strengthen your natural auric protection

- Find a place where you can sit undisturbed
- Choose a color either white, sky blue or gold.
- Carry out the inner light exercise from Chapter 2.
- Close your eyes and imagine or sense that you are creating a bubble of light, extending to about 2 feet around yourself, which is composed of your chosen color. Make sure that this light is above your head, as well as under your feet.
- Sense or imagine this light expanding and contracting until you feel that you have found the most comfortable distance.
- Sense or imagine this light alternating between being stationary and spinning like a top.
- Open your eyes and sense this protection is still around you.
- When you have tried this out with one color, try another.
- Assess which color you feel most comfortable with and note down any other feelings or sensations.

Note: Technically white and gold are not true colors but are included here for the vibrational energy that they reflect.

COLOR AND PROTECTION

If you carried out the protection exercise correctly, you would have noticed that one color felt more appropriate for you than another. I have given this exercise on many occasions to my students and have been struck by how clear their preferences can be. Some individuals feel completely at home with a blue bubble of protection, but averse to gold, while others are aware of an opposite reaction. The reason for this lies in the basic make-up of the person in question. It also highlights the power of color in our imagery world and how we respond to these images in our psyche.

Colors are used in religious and mystical groups to denote different hierarchies or levels of authority: the Bishops, Cardinals and Pope in the Catholic Church wear colored robes to denote their respective offices. The three colors from the protection exercise, white, blue and gold, carry the following meanings:

- **Gold** is associated with the sun and carries a powerful Yang, or positive energy, that can be very forceful. It will consume any energy that is not in harmony with it. Those who have an outgoing, positive outlook on life will find this energy most appropriate. It suits the action people of this world. It is a color that is most appropriate in situations where there is much disturbed energy around.

- **White** symbolizes purity and vitality. It reflects all colors and therefore has the effect of reflecting back whatever is sent at it. It can be very helpful where energies are being projected onto others. Its mirroring quality allows others to begin to see the effects of their thoughts and actions upon us. It is a good color to use in normal day-to-day circumstances and is often the color suggested for protection in books. However, there are some who find its energies too agitating and therefore do not get on well with using it.

- **Sky-blue** is sometimes referred to as Madonna blue and carries a soothing, passive energy that neutralizes and harmonizes what is projected onto it. Its link with the divine feminine archetype and the quality of spiritual love gives it wide appeal. It will tend to transform and diffuse energies in a non-intrusive way. It is the natural color for those whose approach to life is more passive and gentle. However, some individuals feel that it carries a claustrophobic quality that smothers their vitality. This may be caused by difficult associations with one's mother.

These color associations have been established over a long period of time by those who have meditated upon and used color symbolism in their religious practices. These three colors are the primary protectors in the spectrum but other hues can be used, including pink and violet. These have different flavors of energy, which might attract you. The way to find out is by experimentation and noting down what you feel or sense about these qualities.

Getting into this mode of experience is something that women, on the whole, are better at than men. It requires an ability to get out of the intellectual part of your mind and into your feeling, sensing and intuitive aspects. As we proceed through the book, other exercises will be suggested to help this process along. When these connections start to happen it is rather like 'seeing' the picture, for the first time, in those three-dimensional drawings that contain a hidden image. The mind suddenly makes the link and the picture leaps out with startling clarity. The strange thing about psi awareness is when you suddenly discover your ability to be receptive at this other level, you often discover that you have been picking up information all along without realizing it.

SYMBOLS AND PROTECTION

You could liken the psi protective colors to your basic clothes, to which you can add a whole range of protective symbols, such as the cross, that will overlay the color with an additional quality of energy. In a later chapter, more detailed information will be included about the use of symbols but, in essence, symbols act as links to the different flavors of energy described in Chapter 2. Study any Renaissance painting and it is littered with different symbols, each conveying messages from the artist. On a psi level, symbols act as access codes on the quantum plane for specific qualities of energy. Symbols come in four forms. They can be:

- Of human origin, for example a shield.
- Animals, for example a lion.
- Geometric symbols, for example a Star of David.
- Natural or cosmic symbols, for example, a star or water.

When working with symbols, you can imagine that they are over the top of your head, placed next to you (in front, behind, beside, or under your feet) or that you are standing within them. Their energy then becomes linked to you. At the higher grades, all martial arts are based upon the use of energy, or Ch'i, by the mind and the different ways that you can throw your opponent off-balance, by using your energy correctly.

There may be occasions where you feel a difficult energy is coming from one particular individual. In these cases, you may find that imagining a mirror between you and them is most appropriate. This will have the effect of breaking any links that are coming to you.

PROTECTION AT WORK

Protection is important in all areas where there may be difficult energies around. Those in the teaching, police and caring professions are particularly vulnerable, but in practice there are many areas or jobs that have a potentially conflicting dynamic. A few suggestions are given below, connected to different professions, for appropriate symbols to add to your auric color. You can experiment with them to see what feels appropriate.

- Caring professions: caduceus (staff of Hermes) or lotus.
- Teaching or writing: book or quill pen.
- Law: scales.
- Police or armed services: dog or lioness.
- Acting: a lyre.
- Musician: white rose over your head.
- Mediator: lotus under one's body or over the head.

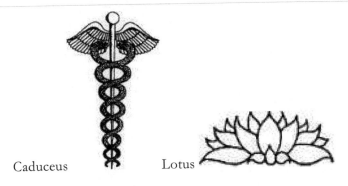

Caduceus   Lotus

These symbols, related to the mythology chart in Chapter 5, give an idea of the different qualities that you might require for any particular activity. Animal symbols such as a lion, bear or dog are good guardians and general protectors whenever you feel physically or mentally threatened by something or someone. The chalice is a symbol of inspiration and should be used whenever you need additional insight. The lotus brings harmony and is excellent for group meetings where confrontations could be destructive.

PROTECTION AROUND OTHER THINGS

Protection can be applied not just to yourself but to any person, place or object that may need psi help. Instead of imagining that you are placing a bubble of light around yourself, visualize it around the object or person that you are thinking about. Some examples of where protections may be appropriate include:

- your home
- your car
- your place of work
- your family members
- your meditation room or space
- your healing or psi development work
- your projects

DOES PROTECTION WORK?

You may ask whether these methods of protection actually work. The proof of the pudding must lie in the eating and only experience will tell whether you will come to value your protection. I have known people who have stepped unhurt out of cars that have been written off in accidents; who have found they could cope with difficult situations where before they felt overwhelmed; who have had their houses broken into but had very little or nothing stolen. In all these cases, the individuals felt that their protection had been of great value. The most dramatic case happened to an individual who owned a farm in Australia.

A bush fire broke out in her area and looked as though it would destroy her home and all her stock. They brought all the animals in close to the property and then this person imagined a strong protection right around their land. The fire came up to the edge of where she had visualized the protection, then split and went around its perimeter before being brought under control. Her land was completely untouched.

I think that psi protection, in conjunction with the energy recharging techniques that will be described in the section on healing, is one of the most effective ways of helping you maintain a healthy and fulfilled life (obviously, other factors such as the food that you eat and your ability to deal with stress are also important). Experience has taught me that those who develop their psi faculty but neglect protection usually hit problems sooner or later. Work with these ideas and they will become very valuable tools.

ADDITIONAL PROTECTION EXERCISE (time: 5 to 10 mins)

Aim: This exercise will allow you to draw upon the creativity of your mind to strengthen your auric protection (rather like trying on different clothes to see which suit)

- Repeat the previous exercise but this time ask within for a color to represent protection.
- Now imagine an animal that symbolizes protection for you. Where would you place the animal in relationship to yourself?
- Next visualize a flower that symbolizes protection. Where does this flower rest in relation to your body?
- Visualize an item of clothing that represents protection and feel yourself wearing this clothing. When would you most need to wear it?
- Finally, slowly bring yourself back to full waking consciousness.
- Note down your response to the symbols and any associations at a mental or emotional level: which did you feel comfortable with and which did you not?

PSI HIGHWAY CODE

Before concluding this chapter, it is important to say a few words on the pitfalls and dangers of using the psi aspect of your being.

In all walks of life, dangers abound. Statistically, most accidents occur in the home, yet we still live in homes because they provide an important function. Sensible precautions will avoid most problems in the home and the situation with psi development is similar. The exercises given in this book are for general use and you should follow the suggestions. If you wish to develop further, then seek out a good teacher; their experience will be of great benefit to you and they will be able to help you integrate within your life what you are exploring.

Do not mix any psi development work with non-prescribed drugs or alcohol. They will distort the psi faculty and could lead to mental or psychological imbalance. Do not try to develop your psi faculty if you are under prescribed medication for mental or psychological problems.

Occasionally, exploring one's inner world will throw up unresolved issues from the past. If problems arise from this, seek help. A list of organizations involved with psi development is given in the appendix.

Exploring these inner gifts can bring immense satisfaction and reward. I don't think it is something to be frightened about, any more than you should be frightened about fitness training or any other creative outlet. Obviously some hobbies have more dangers than others but, approached in a sensible way, psi development will only bring you benefits.

Your Psi Skills:

The Powers Within

CHAPTER 4

Psi Receptivity and Meditation

Your psi faculty is a normal part of you and, like any skill, can be readily developed with a little application. Like musical talent, some people are naturally more gifted than others, but that should not deter you. Unfortunately, children, who are often aware of these other dimensions, are put off by the fears of their parents from expressing what they sense and feel through their psi faculty. A block develops, which needs to be overcome when interest is aroused again in later life.

Every level of your being is a potential receiver of information from outside. In the esoteric thought tradition, there are many bands, each of a finer and finer level of vibration and each mirroring the energies of the other bands. All are connected together through resonance. Within human beings, the simplest way of seeing these bands is to think of four levels: physical, emotional, mental and spiritual. These four levels relate to the four elements of earth (body), water (emotions), air (mind), and fire (spirit). Carl Jung classified them as sensation, feeling, thinking and intuition.

In the psi system, each of these four levels can be used to pick up information: you can pick up psi information through your body, your emotions, your mind or your spiritual self. Different techniques have been traditionally developed to explore these levels of receptivity. For example, dowsing or divining uses the physical body as the main medium for extra sensory perception. Figure 4.1 illustrates the four receptive senses.

In Section 3, these different techniques will be explored more fully, along with a number of exercises. However, to set the scene, the psi aspect of each of these levels is included here.

SENSATIONS

The physical body responds very quickly to the different levels of psi energy within it. Remember the last time that you were angry or upset. Where did you sense the energy in your body? When healers channel energy to their clients, they will often report a sensation of heat or tingling in their hands. Their patients will also sometimes be aware of different sensations in their bodies.

There are two ways that these sensations can be interpreted. Firstly, yes/no responses can be amplified, which is how dowsers operate; secondly, the particular sensation in your body can be interpreted. In this context, healers will sometimes experience pain or discomfort in a particular part of their body which corresponds with the patient's area of imbalance. Often, this will happen without the patient giving any previous information. Effectively, the healers learn to listen to their own bodies to determine where the problems lie for their clients. This aspect of psi is generally known as clairsentience.

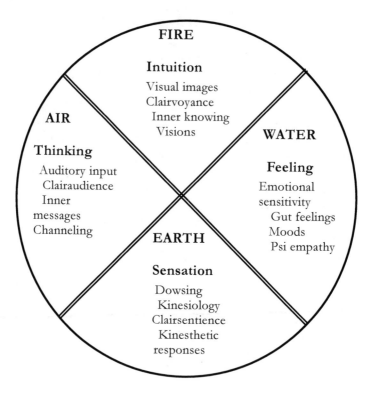

Fig. 4.1 The four receptive senses.

Dowsing techniques involve the use of some instrument, a pendulum, hazel rod or bent coat hanger, to amplify very slight muscle reactions. This system is used to gain a yes/no answer to a question. Diviners looking for water have an idea in their minds of what they are seeking; they then rely on their bodies to do the rest. If their minds and bodies are connected at the inner level, then slight muscle twitches will be amplified through the rods, telling them when they have hit water. A good diviner can program his or her mind to pick up anything, from a lost object, to oil, gold or buried treasure. This ability is not restricted to site visits but can be shown to be just as effective when working from maps.

Many people have had a go at using a pendulum that responds to slight movements of the hand. It is not the pendulum that picks up information; it is you. All the pendulum does is amplify what you know within you. These are not difficult techniques to learn and they will be fully covered in later chapters.

FEELINGS

The psi feeling response can best be summed up by the words 'gut reactions'. Interestingly, in Ancient Chinese culture, the seat of intelligence was said to be the abdominal area, which is why Chinese statues sometimes have huge pot bellies. Feelings involve all your emotions and can give insights into the underlying causes of any situations. When I started my psi development, many years ago, I often got stuck when trying to bring forward clairvoyant images. They just would not come, until I hit upon the idea of asking myself, 'What do I feel about this object, situation or problem?' Immediately, I would get a response. Many therapists use this faculty when working with their clients as the subtle changes in the feeling response can be picked up quickly. If you are a person who responds easily to the moods of others, it is likely that this faculty is working well within you and you can develop it as part of your psi training.

THINKING

At first glance, thinking may not seem to be an aspect of psi receptivity. After all, we are thinking most of the time, and this has little to do with picking up subtle levels of information. However, your mind can be used in three ways in the psi system.

The first involves hearing an inner voice giving you information. This inner voice, which is generally an aspect of your psi consciousness, translates its information into verbal information that can be easily understood. This is sometimes referred to as clairaudience in psychic development circles. One of the challenges here is that the rational part of the mind will often step in to refute what has been said, particularly if it defies normal logic. An example of this occurred to me when I was standing next to a tree which, in my imagination, then started to talk to me about its role in nature. All good, fanciful, stuff until it said that it had been instrumental in helping a particular friend of mine who had been going through a very difficult emotional crisis. Here was a wonderful opportunity to test the validity of the message: all I needed to do was to ask my friend if this was true. I had hardly started to tell her about the experience when she said that she knew the tree I meant. On one particular day, in extreme distress, she had spent several hours crying her heart out under the tree and had a strange sensation that somehow it had actually helped her. Make of this story what you will, but I can vouch that I did not know beforehand that this had happened.

To some people, hearing inner voices can be very disturbing. It could well be that this is an aspect receptive psi faculties that has not been balanced or integrated within their psyches.

Another form of this method of psi communication is channeling, which has become very popular in some groups in recent years. In these situations the channeler enters into a semi-trance and then allows another level of consciousness, whether it be another spirit or higher aspect of themselves, to speak through them. I have used this method myself on many occasions and the relayed information can be very insightful and helpful for the participants who are hearing the message.

'Automatic writing' is another aspect of this category of psi function. This is achieved by simply sitting with a question in mind and then allowing yourself to write a response without any logical interference from the conscious mind. You are in effect tapping into what Carl Jung called the 'collective unconscious' which is full of creative ideas and solutions. Sometimes people use this method to connect with deceased ancestors as a way of resolving family dynamics that have their origin in some past trauma. You allow the 'ancestor' to convey their messages through the writing.

The final way that the thinking psi function works is through creative ideas. Obviously we all have an inner level of assessment that can take a problem and sort it through to bring forward a creative thought. Sometimes, these thoughts have a quality of being outside our normal thinking patterns, rather as though we are accessing a much greater information database. Those thoughts that sometimes come out of the blue carrying a powerful inspirational idea could be examples of this function at work.

INTUITION

Your intuitional mode is closest in vibrational terms to the spiritual self. It communicates best through visual imagery and an inner knowing that can be very powerful. In psi terms, dreams are seen as a reflection of this layer of inner communication, which is why some dreams contain prophetic material.

The term clairvoyance is used to describe the imagery aspect of this mode. A clairvoyant practitioner will put his or her mind into a form of free flow and watch the different pictures that emerge from the deeper layers of consciousness. In essence, it is very similar to day-dreaming, except that the clairvoyant is trying to elicit specific information about a subject and the day-dreamer is happy for his or her mind to wander at will. The pictures that emerge are then interpreted either by the clairvoyant or the client or some other person.

The pictures from the clairvoyant mind can be of two forms: either symbolic or factual. Confusion can arise if you do not know which is which. For example, a student was sending healing to a client sat in front them when they inwardly perceived an image of a giant wood-cutting saw, and became very conscious of the teeth of this saw. At first glance, these images appeared to have no connection with the patient who was not involved in forestry and any such pursuit. The healer's mind was in fact conveying the fact that her patient had 'sore teeth'; the patient then confirmed this, stating that she had had many operations since childhood on her teeth and gums. This information had not been passed to the healer before she started the treatment; it was her clairvoyant mind that told her where the healing was required.

Some people find visualization difficult but practice and patience will help. You do not have to have brilliant clarity for visual images to work. The following exercise will give you a taste of how well your visual mind operates.

VISUALIZATION EXERCISES (time: 5 mins)

Aim: To assess the ability of your mind to produce visual images

- Adopt your normal meditation pose or sit comfortably in an upright chair and relax.
- Think of an object that is very familiar to you, such as your car or the front of your house.
- Close your eyes and try to visualize that object in as much detail as you can, listing at least ten points that you notice.
- Open your eyes and go and look at what you were visualizing to see how accurate your inner picture was.
- Give yourself marks out of ten for the clarity of the images that came to you.

You could practice this exercise every day for the next week and access how much your visualization ability improves. If you thought of your car and could assess its color and general shape then you are at least on the starting grid for developing your visualization ability. Assessing whether your mind works better with symbolism or factual images will take a bit of time and practice.

MEDITATION TECHNIQUES

There are many different systems of meditation in the world today, some very ancient and some that have been developed recently. The goal of meditation should be to help integrate the spiritual dimension into the rest of your life and to balance your psi energies. In Hindu and Buddhist tradition, the exclusive development of psi powers, or 'siddhis' as they are known, was not approved of; they are acceptable, however, as an integrated part of spiritual seeking. Meditation can help the process of self-healing and spiritual integration.

In broad terms, meditation techniques can be classified as either dynamic or passive. Dynamic meditations work with the mind in a creative way, often using symbolic images to access the deeper layers of consciousness. Guided imagery meditations, which have become popular recently, come into this category. Prayer is really a form of dynamic meditation in which specific help is being invoked in a direct way.

Passive meditations try to put the mind into a neutral state so that the deeper impressions of the psyche merge with the conscious mind, but in a non-intrusive way. It has been well recognized how easily the rational mind gets in the way and many techniques have been developed to bypass its clouded outlook.

Both dynamic and passive meditations have their place and one is not better than the other. Ideally, you need to find the systems that best suit your temperament. This is important and will depend upon a number of factors. As a generalization, the Eastern approach to spiritual seeking tends to be passive, whereas in the West the dynamic approach is more dominant.

THE IMPORTANCE OF MEDITATION

A few years ago, I had the opportunity of interviewing Drukchen Rinpoche, one of the important Lamas from Tibet who perceives himself as a direct incarnation of Avolokitsvara, the Tibetan Buddha of Compassion.

When I asked Drukchen about meditation, he affirmed its importance in the spiritual life. When questioned further on how long we should meditate for, he said, surprisingly, 'No more than five minutes per day.' Going on, he said, 'People are crazy and meditation can make you more crazy.' The most important aspect of meditation for him was holding the focus of your mind on the subject of your meditation. As he stated 'It is far better to spend five minutes in concentrated thought rather than fifty minutes in mindless drift.' Meditation does not, therefore, need to take up a lot of time but can be easily incorporated into your schedule. Normally, I will spend five minutes every morning and evening in meditation and only extend this period if there is specific information that I am trying to access, understand or balance within me. Indeed, seen in a different way, if meditation is directed to allowing the spiritual self full expression within us, then your whole life could become a form of meditation.

One simple meditation/concentration exercise is included here which can be linked to the other exercises in this book. A number of good books on meditation are listed in the Appendix.

CONCENTRATION EXERCISES (time: 3 to 5 mins)

Aim: **To develop your concentration and visualization ability**

You will require a candle and timer for this exercise.

- Light the candle and sit in one of the poses described previously.
- Set the timer for two minutes.
- With your eyes open, focus your mind on the candle as a shape and object only. Observe its colors, the energy of the flame and how it relates to the background, but nothing else. If your mind starts to wander off or make connections to other things, gently bring it back to the candle. If you are unused to doing this, two minutes will seem a long time.
- When the two minutes are over, re-establish contact with your normal waking mode.
- Next, set the timer for two minutes again, but this time in looking at the candle allow your mind to contemplate how it was made, what candles are used for, why they are often part of religious rites, what they symbolize, etc. Allow whatever associations that come up to be explored but keep coming back to the candle.
- When the two minutes are up, once more re-establish contact with your normal waking mode.
- Finally, set the timer again, but this time close your eyes and try to visualize the candle for two minutes. If the image starts to fade, briefly open your eyes, look at it again, and then repeat trying to visualize it.
- Once again re-establish contact with your normal waking mode when the time is up. Then write down your impressions.

If you carry out any of these exercises within a group, share your experiences, as it can be very valuable to perceive other insights.

This type of exercise can be carried out with many different types of objects, a pencil, your hand, a piece of sculpture, to name but a few. When you feel ready, you can extend the time of each session to 3, 4 or 5 minutes. This will help your healing work and strengthen your ability to hold the focus of your attention at will.

The next exercises are adapted from my book, *The Healer Within*, and will help you develop your meditational techniques.

This type of meditation will provide powerful insights into many facets of life. You can use this form of identification exercise with almost anything: animals, plants, buildings (pyramid), people (Christ/Buddha), fish, stars, symbols and so on. Your mind has an infinite capacity to bring forth all sorts of associations and perceptions that can be of real value in helping you link with your spiritual side.

MERGING EXERCISES (time: 5 mins)

Aim: To give greater awareness of other life forms in nature and how they relate to you. In this exercise a tree is chosen but any aspect of nature can be used.

- Adopt your normal meditation pose, close your eyes and carry out the body awareness exercise.
- Next, imagine that you are standing in front of a tree. You have no shoes or stockings on so that you can feel the ground beneath your feet. Be aware of any sounds that you can hear, of birds or insects. There is a gentle breeze blowing and you can feel its soft caress on your cheek. Look at the shape and size of the tree. What type of tree is it? Now move closer and feel its bark. Is it rough or smooth?
- Next, turn your back to the tree and feel yourself leaning against it. What feelings do you get from this tree? What is this type of tree used for? Can you see the processes of its use in your mind?
- Now, finally let yourself start to merge with the tree, so that you become it and it becomes you, feeling up into its branches and down to the roots. What do you now experience? Allow yourself to be in this space for a minute or two, before disengaging. See yourself once more as separate from the tree, standing looking at it. Then let the picture fade your mind and be aware of yourself again in the room and open your eyes.
- Write down what you have experienced.

The above exercise is particularly helpful in producing a sense of calm and well-being, particularly when going through any stressful situation. It does, however, require a discipline, both in setting aside time and in focusing on the images. When stressful situations arise, there is often a tendency to worry endlessly and churn over the problem in your mind. Re-directing your thoughts in other directions through meditation require a discipline of the mind, which is not easy, but if successfully applied be enormously beneficial.

The trick in this form of meditation is to bring into play as many of your physical senses as you can. In other words, see what you inwardly observe in the scene you create, listen for any sounds, feel any sensations in your body and smell any scents. For example if you choose a scene in the middle of a forest, try to see the different trees, touch their barks and sense the different textures, either rough or smooth; listen out for the sound of bird song or the wind rustling through the leaves; smell the musty scent of the earth. If you can bring into play at least three of these senses, your whole mind will be focused in the meditation.

Finally, we are all made up of both balanced and chaotic elements, the light and shadowy aspects of our beings. Both are important in our development. You should never try to run away from those aspects that you find disagreeable within; if you do, they are liable to overwhelm you in one way or another. The shadow contains all the unacknowledged parts of you as well as anger, greed, fear and so on. Sometimes, when carrying out any meditation, the shadowy elements will emerge. Do not be frightened of them. Acknowledge them, experience them but do not identify with them. Underlying all destructive emotions is fear in one form or another. To be whole, you cannot run away from this fear. In truth, the only thing you have to fear is the fear itself. Sit with it, experience it, and then move through it into wholeness.

QUIET PLACE MEDITATION (time: 5 mins)

Aim: To help you find peace and tranquility within

- Think of a place, either in the country or by the sea, where you have felt very calm and peaceful. Visualize yourself at that place, experiencing all that you did before. Look around and try to see everything as it was then. Listen out for any sounds of birds or insects and the smell of grass or flowers. Above all, use your sense of touch to feel the bark of any trees, the lapping water or the ground beneath you.

- Adopt your normal meditation posture, close your eyes and carry out your body awareness exercise.

- Now imagine that you are sitting or walking in this place. Use as many of your physical senses as you can. Above all, recall the feeling of peace and tranquility that you experienced and allow it to permeate every cell of your body.

- When you feel you have been in this state for a few minutes, slowly disengage and bring yourself back to full waking consciousness.

CHAPTER 5

The Universities of the Mind: Myths, Archetypes and Symbols

This is an enormous subject on which whole books could be written. Spiritual seeking and psi development have been around for a very long time. The experiences of those who have explored and developed their psi gifts in the past have created pathways, or gateways, into the psi quantum realm, which make it that little bit easier for us to travel along behind them. In this chapter we will explore two main themes. Firstly, the significance of myths and how, in conjunction with symbols, they can be used to enhance your skills and inner awareness. Secondly, how a consistent set of spiritual principles is reflected in all cultures.

THE SIGNIFICANCE OF MYTHS

Myths and fairy stories are found in all societies and attempt to convey information about the weaving together of spiritual forces and how they integrate into the human world. They were created to help individuals understand their place within the cosmos. The advancement of scientific knowledge in the twentieth century has, in some ways, tended to relegate myths to the status of stories of superstitious people with little relevance for human consciousness. In adopting this stance, we can easily miss the insights that the myths convey.

'As above, so below' was one of the Hermetic axioms of the ancient wisdom tradition. In other words, the creative patterns of the cosmos are reflected down through every level of experience from the spiritual to the physical. Science has been highly successful in establishing and understanding the physical laws that hold this world in place. For example scientists have been able to provide evidence on why the 'law of gravity' operates in the same way throughout the world. Newton's falling apple, and the scientific laws determining its descent, is the same in Tibet, America or China. Despite a few anomalies, it is the consistency of science which gives it its strength.

However, when we turn to spiritual beliefs, there appears to be a plethora of differing views in the way that individuals and religions operate. Regrettably, this can even lead to conflict. Yet in delving beneath the surface of these different traditions, many similarities do emerge which can provide important insights into the function of different spiritual forces. Myths give us clues to the way past cultures understood and worked with these 'other-dimensional' energies. If the axiom, 'As above, so below' is correct, then we would expect to find that a set of coherent universal laws and patterns exist on every level from the spiritual to the physical. When we approach the myths and stories from this perspective, looking for the underlying patterns or connections, many of the seeming differences melt away.

In more modern times mythic stories like 'Harry Potter' or 'Lord of the Rings' have captured people's imaginations. Children today, with access to computers, can enter into and participate in fantasy games involving many mythological creatures. Why are such stories so potent? Strange as it may seem it is my perception that these epics tap into specific archetypal themes and characters that portray the workings of archetypal forces within the spiritual realm. This is a concept we will return to again.

We are now at the start of the twenty-first century and science and mysticism are beginning to move closer to each other. Having removed God from all scientific concepts in the nineteenth century, the idea of some creative intelligence behind the cosmos is not now so readily derided. There are aspects of the physical world, such as the near-death experience and psi phenomena, that cannot be explained in terms of known physical laws. God or some type of formative directed intelligence is once more entering the picture for some scientists.

So let us start by assuming that there is some type of overseeing Creative Intelligence behind the universe which has formulated a series of 'laws' that holds the physical and spiritual worlds in place. I have already discussed one such apparently universal law - that of polarity - which is expressed by the ancient Chinese concept of Yang and Yin and found even in the smallest particles of the material world. An Intelligence that can both generate and be responsible for the whole cosmos must be of a supreme order. To be able to connect to all aspects of life, it would have to establish links that access every level of experience within the universe. Here the metaphor of the Internet can help us understand how this might operate.

I have already postulated that psi could be seen as an aspect of a 'quantum' global highway, a web of information that links people together through their minds. Through the internet the latest thinking, no matter how bizarre, is available to us. Let us suppose that the quantum psi highway has the same inter-connecting function. In addition, within its vast network there exists a number of 'universities' that are repositories of knowledge and wisdom linked to the Supreme Intelligence or Intelligences that stand behind this universe. Suppose that this system has been in existence since the dawn of creation and was used by peoples of the past to gain insight and knowledge of the world in which they lived. To connect to these 'Halls of Learning', all that was needed was the correct access codes. What might these be? It is my perception that the evidence for this abounds in mythology.

I have already discussed how the quantum psi realm can be accessed best through visual imagery. I would speculate here that this is why mythological and religious stories are rich in symbolism. Many religious groups also use a wide variety of symbolic images in the representation of their beliefs. These images help the mind focus upon and connect to the relevant spiritual energies and the wisdom that they contain. In religious terms, an image of the Madonna will help a Christian focus his or her prayers in a meaningful way, whereas a Taoist might pray to the goddess Kwan Yin. In essence, the energy behind these two beings is very similar, representing compassion and mercy.

We do not even have to go to religion to recognize the power of symbolic images. Advertising is based far more on what is presented visually than what is spoken or written. Logos and symbols access the deeper recesses of the mind and connect us to some very interesting informational patterns. Computers also use similar ideas: symbols are generally used instead of words for different commands.

THE UNIVERSITIES OF CONSCIOUS

To make life easier let us suppose that there are a small number of principle universities, on a spiritual level, each linked to the supreme intelligence we call God. Each university has a slightly different function and is responsible for exploring or expressing a facet of universal truth. As in a physical university, there would be some overlap in research work, and all would be linked together. Knowing the correct access codes would allow you to gain whatever information you might require. The only proviso would be that you would only be able to gather information consistent with the level of your present knowledge in the same way that a child's question to a professor on a particular subject would get a very different answer from a similar question posed by an adult.

It is my belief that the myths and their stories tell us all about these different universities, as seen through the eyes of those who worked within them in the past. In attempting to interpret this information, we have to be mindful that what we see today is a blurred picture, because any group will subjectively understand and connect to these repositories of knowledge from its own particular point of view, on the basis of the needs of the community at that time. Times and circumstances have changed greatly; the spiritual needs and understanding of the world are very different today from what they were in the past. We urgently need new models to make these connections. Fortunately, there have been many wise teachers and spiritual leaders who have opened the pages of this quantum realm and conveyed what they saw. In reading their accounts, we can appreciate the nature and quality of what they have accessed and, more importantly, it provides us with the opportunity of unlocking this knowledge once more for ourselves.

To ground this idea further and based on my explorations into the psi quantum realm, I suggest here that there are eight primary universities that operate through the spiritual realm associated with human life. In the past, individuals perceived these universities of creative consciousness either as their gods or goddesses or through symbols, such as the trigrams of the I Ching. A better way to look at them today is as doorways to a global university network of 'higher' consciousness. I have chosen eight because this reflects the 8 trigrams of the I Ching and, as we shall see, can be shown to be reflected in different mythological systems.

In Figure 5.1, I have listed the relationships between these universities and how they were depicted in some of the ancient mythologies. The chart is not meant to be comprehensive but is given as a guide to show you how you can cross-reference these archetypal patterns through different mythologies. To translate these ideas into everyday language, I have also drawn a parallel with a traditional company structure. In other words, we could say that one university relates to marketing, one to finance and so on. Like normal universities, each will have a chancellor and a hierarchy of individuals, professors, administrators and so on who are responsible for the different departments.

ACCESSING THE UNIVERSITIES OF CONSCIOUSNESS

In essence, gaining information from any of these universities can be looked at in a similar way to the acquisition of knowledge through the Internet. You type into 'Google' or some other search engine your request and await a reply. Back comes a long list of sites that give some information on the theme of your request. You have to sift the answers and some of the pages you may not fully trust. You determine what makes sense to you. On the quantum psi highway of the mind, the replies that you receive have to come either through your mind or be translated into some event within your life. One of the immediate problems is that your mind is not used to picking up this information or, perhaps worse, will block out what it does not wish to hear. So the first step is being able to gather 'clearly' what is relayed back to you. Fortunately, there are a number of tried and tested methods that help deal with this difficulty. These will be fully described in Section 3.

It should be stressed that these universities of 'higher consciousness' are available to all who have the time or patience to make the connections. It does not require a great intellect, only a willingness to

Primary qualities	Greek pantheon	Egyptian pantheon	Teutonic/Arthurian	Chinese I Ching	Symbols	Colors	Chakras	Animals	Other attributes
Initiation 1	Zeus Hestia	Osiris	Thor (Donar) Galahad	Ch'ien Father	Gold Crown	Magenta Gold	Crown	Lion Tiger Horse	Philosophy, universal brotherhood, unity, leadership
Transformation 2	Hera Ares	Seth	Loki Morgan Le Fey	K'an Middle son	Cube Square Crescent	Red Dark green	Base	Pig Rat Bat Pegasus	Danger, courage, hardship, cleansing, baptism, force, transformation
Exploration 3	Hades Demeter	Anubis	Heimdall Gawain	Ken Youngest son	Column Pillar	Orange Dark blue	Solar Plexus	Dog White owl	Stillness, research, inner perception, discovery
Formation 4	Apollo Artemis	Horus	Tyr (Tiw)	Li Middle daughter	Eye Pentangle Lyre	Yellow	Throat	Falcon Eagle Swan	Clarity, beauty expressed through arts, crafts and business organisations
Communication 5	Hermes	Thoth	Odin (Wodan) Merlin	Chen Eldest son	Triangle Pyramid Feather Caduceus	Green	Feet	Ibis Monkey Snake	Arousing, growth and evolution, karma, truth, justice, law
Organization 6	Aphrodite Hephaestus	Isis	Freyja Guinevere	K'un Mother	Ankh Star of David	Lilac Madonna blue Turquoise	Heart	Dove Deer Unicorn	Spiritual lore, selfless giving, gentleness
Contemplation 7	Poseidon Persephone	Nephys	Frigg Lady of the Lake	Sun Eldest daughter	Circle Chalice Lotus	Indigo Pink Light green	Sacral	Fish Dolphin	Reflection, revelation, psychic receptivity
Innovation 8	Athene	Hathor	Balder Arthur	Tui Youngest daughter	Cross in circle Flaming sword White rose	Violet White Electric blue	Brow	Lioness Cow Cat Elephant	Joy, protection, spiritual nourishment intuition, insight

Fig. 5.1 Mythology comparison chart

put in your request with an open mind. What comes back will be tailored to your particular need, either as a direct message or as a life event.

Seeking help into some facet of life gets a much greater response than asking to win the lottery. The spiritual intelligences behind these universities are very good judges of what serves your best interests. In my inner exploration and working connection with these universities of the mind I am very aware of a hierarchy of spiritual beings that direct them, very like any terrestrial organization. Individual requests get individual attention and answers. Just as a bank manager will make a calculated assessment before giving you a loan, so will sincere requests to the universities of consciousness, within the quantum realm, be carefully assessed. The more that what you seek can be used for the betterment of other individuals and the world as a whole, the greater will be the level of support and co-operation that you will receive. This can be applied to aspects of your life in all sorts of simple and down-to-earth ways: how you deal with your job, family, friends, and finances can all be helped by accessing this quantum realm of the mind. Having the correct access codes, knowing which of these eight universities best suits your purpose, will speed up and strengthen the responses that you obtain. Accessing your psi internet can also be fun.

SPIRITUAL TEACHERS

Great spiritual teachers across all religions are individuals who have been able to access different facets of this 'quantum' spiritual realm. They have been able to express insights into the spiritual principles that underpin different aspects of life. In my perception the origins of their insights stems from accessing one or other of these spiritual universities, which has leant a particular flavor to their teachings. This is independent of their cultural background. For example the teachings of the Buddha carry a different emphasis from that of Jesus or again Confucius. As an alternative to connecting through a symbol, many individuals prefer to link with an image of their teacher. This is a perfectly good method of opening up to information from this other dimension. Find the right teacher and they will help you both consciously and unconsciously to make these higher dimensional connections. It does not really matter which system you adopt.

THE EIGHT UNIVERSITIES OF THE MIND

In order to create a map so that you can understand the role of these universities and access their various departments, it is necessary to give them names. The easiest way to do this is to ascribe to each a color and a single descriptive word which reflects their different qualities. The ideas given below barely touch the surface of the information available to us through these inner 'Halls of Learning'. They and the chart in Fig. 5.2 are intended as guides to start the process of opening up the enormous potential that lies within. For the moment they are described in a set order that reflects their numeric and color association but in principle they can be arranged in many different ways. Within this book they will later be set out in accordance with patterns established in Ancient China based on the I Ching and Feng Shui.

1. INITIATION (Wisdom) - Magenta

The first university is connected to all aspects of wisdom, motivation, direction, leadership and spiritual seeking. It is linked to all the mythological creator gods such as Osiris and Zeus. It is the principle that initiates new ideas and concepts. In the I Ching (see Chapter 13) it is the Father principle and is associated with kings, presidents, chairmen and the governments of countries, organizations and groups.

- **Associated occupations:** Statesman, politician, monarch, judge, religious seeker, priest, clergyman, head of an organization, leader, own boss.
- **Key access symbol:** Golden crown.
- **Psychological association:** Father
- **Angelic association:** Divine Father
- **Animal symbols:** Lion, bear.

2. TRANSFORMATION (Courage) - Red

This can often be a difficult university to connect with for it invariably brings up the shadow aspects of our personality and confronts us with our deepest fears or those things that we most loathe. If these are not tackled correctly, this energy can distort and introvert, causing a disruptive quality to emerge. This is why most mythologies contain a god or goddess who rebels against the rest; for example the god Set in Egyptian mythology or Loki in Norse. In modern myths this force is portrayed by Sauron in Lord of the Rings or Voldermort in Harry Potter. In the I Ching, this trigram is called K'an and is associated with danger, hardship and evil and how we cope with these aspects of our lives. It needs to be appreciated that this force is necessary because it makes us confront what we most fear and what we most loathe within ourselves.

Its transformational quality is best perceived through the symbol of the white winged horse Pegasus that was born from the head of Medusa. The stellar constellation of Pegasus interestingly sits between the zodiac signs of Pisces and Aquarius and is particularly relevant in these transformational times.

We have to negotiate the transformational energies involved in facing the shadowy aspects of our personalities. Change and transformation are being forced on many businesses at present.

- **Associated occupations:** Psychotherapist, reformer, sociologist, soldier, policeman, prison warden, dictator, sex therapist, prostitute, criminal.
- **Key access symbol:** Pegasus or white winged horse

- **Psychological association:** Shadow
- **Angelic association:** Lucifer
- **Animal symbols:** Pegasus, pig, peacock.

3. EXPLORATION (Faith) - Orange

This university deals with all aspects of research, experimentation and investigation. It is the great explorer of the group, seeking out knowledge and information from every direction. It can also be used when objects or possessions are lost: asking for help will, in most cases, bring a very quick response. St. Anthony carries this energy in Christianity. It is linked to the research and development sections of companies and to all exploration into the mind and psyche. The Egyptian god Anubis, who assisted the souls of the departed into the next dimension, is associated with this university.

- **Associated occupations:** Psychologist, parapsychologist, explorer, scientist, researcher, investigator, detective, archaeologist, funeral director, hospice nurse.
- **Key access symbol:** White Owl.
- **Psychological association:** Guide
- **Angelic association:** Uriel
- **Animal symbols:** Dog, white owl.

4. FORMATION (Clarity) - Yellow

Methods for bringing ideas into reality are contained with this university, which is also linked to production and finance. It is associated with the Egyptian hawk-headed god Horus, who sees his goal clearly; with the Greek god Apollo, who shoots arrows to ground his ideas and acts as patron to the arts, and with the archangel Gabriel in Christianity. It helps bring clarity and single-mindedness to ideas, which can then be important for getting them launched, but also needs to be balanced. Its qualities help projects grow in the most appropriate way.

- **Associated occupations:** Financier, businessman, entrepreneur, artist, designer, architect, builder, engineer, athlete, actor, orator.
- **Key access symbols:** Lyre, golden eye or golden pentangle.
- **Psychological association:** Ego
- **Angelic association:** Gabriel
- **Animal symbols:** Eagle, hawk, swan.

5. COMMUNICATION (Integrity) - Green

This university relates to all aspects of accumulated knowledge, teaching and communication. It is connected to Hermes, the messenger of the Greek gods, to the Egyptian god Thoth, lord of letters, truth and karma, and to the archangel Raphael. Thoth was also associated with magical practices, particularly in relation to health and healing. Interestingly, as well as his winged sandals and hat, Hermes also carries the caduceus, the symbol of which the medical profession still uses today. Travel is also an aspect of this university.

It is also associated with magical practices, which is why the Merlin archetype is so potent and found its way into Lord of the Rings as Gandalf and Harry Potter as Professor Dumbledore.

- **Associated occupations:** Teacher, lecturer, professor, solicitor, barrister, travel agent, publisher, journalist, writer, librarian, doctor, dentist, vet, healer, salesman.
- **Key access symbols:** Book, caduceus or pyramid.
- **Psychological association:** Healer
- **Angelic association:** Raphael
- **Animal symbols:** Baboon, ibis, crow

6. ORGANISATION (Harmony) - Blue

This university is ruled over by the great mother goddesses such as Isis and Kwan Yin and is connected to the energy of love, protection, harmony and care. At a practical level, its energies are reflected in organizational structures and in the way that different departments relate to each other. It is related to the amount of care and attention to detail that we give to others, or to our work or pleasure activities. Organizations can tend to become static, so the qualities of its opposite sign of change and transformation become important in helping to maintain balance. In Egypt, Isis was one of the most important mother goddesses, using her magical power to resurrect her husband Osiris. In Christianity, this role has been associated with the Madonna.

- **Associated occupations:** Nurse, carer, midwife, administrator, secretary, personnel officer, charity worker, factory worker, arbitrator, housewife, gardener, landscape architect.
- **Key access symbols:** Lily of the Valley, Ankh.
- **Psychological association:** Mother
- **Angelic association:** Divine Mother
- **Animal symbols:** Dove, deer.

7. REFLECTION (Peace) - Indigo

This university relates to all aspects of inner tranquility and retrospection. It is best exemplified by the poise on the face of the Buddha. In Greek mythology, this energy was understood in terms of the god Dionysus, in the Arthurian it is the Lady of the Lake and in Lord of the Rings Galadriel. All substances that cause altered states of consciousness, such as alcohol, drugs and medicines, are a physical expression of this university. On a practical level, recreation, pastimes and pleasurable pursuits are associated with it. All mystical pursuits come under this university.

- **Associated occupations:** Recreationalist, monk, nun, hermit, vintner, publican, pharmacist, psychic consultant.
- **Key access symbols:** Lotus (water lily), chalice.
- **Psychological Association:** Observer
- **Angelic association:** Cassiel
- **Animal symbols:** Fish, dolphin.

8. INNOVATION (Vision) - Violet

The last of our universities relates to all aspects of invention, innovation and vision. It is therefore primarily associated with intuition, insight and creativity. It is connected with the Greek goddess Athene, who was born from the head of her father Zeus, symbolically indicating the link with the intuitional mind. This is the primary university for anyone who needs to find a new angle or way of approaching a problem. The challenge is how to ground these ideas in the physical world and the answer to this lies in its opposite sign. In Christianity this university is connected to the archangel Michael who wields a flaming sword, and to the cow-headed goddess Hathor in Egyptian mythology, who is associated with joy and nourishment. Hathor was one of the supreme goddesses and was married to Horus (Formation); she could also change form into the warrior goddess Sekhmet, symbolized by the lioness. Innovators and creators in all walks of life should draw consciously on the energies of this university.

- **Associated occupations:** Inventor, innovator, planner, forecaster, visionary, musician, chef, restaurateur, hotelier.
- **Key access symbols:** White Rose or Cross within a Circle.
- **Psychological Association:** Child
- **Angelic association:** Michael
- **Animal symbols:** Lioness, cow, unicorn.

COMPLETING THE PATTERN

The easiest way to see ourselves connecting to these universities is to place ourselves in the centre of the pattern. This is the way it was done in Bagua of Ancient China, which was based on a magic square containing all of the numbers between 1 and 9. The initiatory path that we all have to undertake at some level is to learn to confront our fears and to redeem and transform the aspects of our being that we find unacceptable. Carl Jung called this the path of Individuation.

To successfully carry out this quest we have to call upon help from 'higher dimensions'. We can do this by connecting directly to these 'quantum universities' or by general prayer, which is why balanced spiritual belief is important to our psychological wellbeing.

- **Occupations:** The initiatory journey of the hero and heroine in connecting to their 'higher wisdom'. The path of Individuation.
- **Key access symbols:** Sun or star
- **Psychological Association:** Self

Making Connections

There are a number of ways that you can begin to access the universities of the quantum realm. The following series of exercises will show you how to access the information and help that you can obtain from each of these universal energies.

Building a Color Wheel

Cut out some gummed paper in the seven colors of the spectrum, plus magenta, into triangles and circles and stick them onto a sheet of white paper in the pattern shown in Fig. 5.3. This will act as a focus for your inner connection. Some people find it easier to work with the colors in a circle; others prefer them in a line across the page. You can experiment with both.

- To build up an inner picture for accessing the different universities, close your eyes and try to visualize or sense the position and shape of the different colors. You do not have to 'see' them clearly, just a sense of the position and color will do.
- When you connect to a color, imagine that a golden thread is linking you to it rather like a fine telephone line. For example, while writing this book I have been connected to the 'Green' university (writing and communication) and new insights and information have come forward.

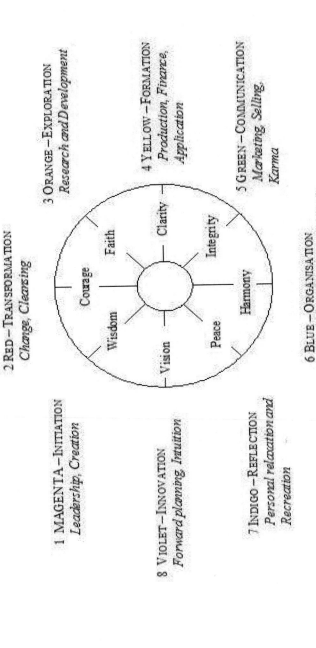

2 RED – TRANSFORMATION
Change, Cleansing

3 ORANGE – EXPLORATION
Research and Development

4 YELLOW – FORMATION
*Production, Finance,
Application*

5 GREEN – COMMUNICATION
*Marketing, Selling,
Karma*

6 BLUE – ORGANISATION
*Administration Personnel and
Arbitration*

7 INDIGO – REFLECTION
*Personal relaxation and
Recreation*

8 VIOLET – INNOVATION
Forward planning Intuition

1 MAGENTA – INITIATION
Leadership, Creation

Courage
Faith
Clarity
Integrity
Wisdom
Vision
Peace
Harmony

Fig. 5.2 The Quantum University Wheel

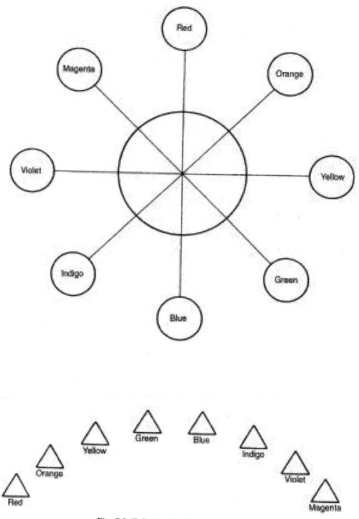

Fig. 5.3 Colour wheel and template.

Every problem has an answer and if nothing appears to happen, that in itself may be the answer. I have never yet posed a question that does not get some reply, but I know that at times I have had to be patient.

WHICH UNIVERSITY SHOULD I LINK TO?

The listings shown above indicate the broad categories that are covered by each 'university' or archetypal grouping. Select the university based upon the specifics of what is being requested.

If the lists of subjects covered by each university do not help you decide, then ask the 'Orange' university for help, as this university can direct calls to their correct destination.

HEALTH ISSUES AND THE UNIVERSITIES

Health issues are covered by a number of universities, depending upon the situation. The following list gives some suggestions:

1. Magenta University: Spiritual problems and issues to do with your father.
2. Red University: This is the realm of psychotherapists, psychologists and those issues dealing with psychological personality problems such as depression and schizophrenia. Sexual problems are also covered by this university.
3. Orange University: Relates to death and dying and helping souls make a good transition into the spirit world.
4. Yellow University: Primarily covers issues to do with your place in the world. It is very helpful for grounding, self assertiveness and dealing with practical issues.
5. Green University: Deals with karmic issues as well as all areas that require balance, which is why the 'caduceus', the symbol of the medical profession is connected to this university. Ancestral healing is also a part of this university.
6. Blue University: Covers all relationship problems and issues. It is the university that should be invoked to help bring forgiveness to any situation. It also relates to all emotional problems and particularly to difficult mother issues.
7. Indigo University: Helps deal with all stress related illnesses. Its calming quality can bring great relief when confronting stressful situations. Into this category also come insights into the origins of health issues, which often stem from some emotional trauma. Psychic receptivity and mediumship and their attendant problems are also covered here.
8. Violet University: Relates particularly to the 'inner child' and unresolved childhood issues. As these qualities are often important in creativity all aspects of intuition come under this domain.

This list gives some broad ideas but is not conclusive. You can always check which university is most appropriate by using one of the techniques, such as dowsing which are described in Section 3 of this book.

ACCESSING YOU INNER UNIVERSITY (time: 5 to 10 mins)

Aim: To gain information and help from the quantum universities

Method 1:

• Think of a question or some aspect of your life that needs help.

• Carry out the body awareness exercise and connect to your inner light.

• Visualize the colored chart in the exercise above and ask the right color for the situation to stand out.

• Imagine that you are connected to that color via a golden thread to the top of your head.

• Ask your question and be open to receiving whatever information comes back to you.

• At this point, you may receive information in line with the four levels indicated in the preceding chapter. Do not be worried if nothing happens immediately.

• When you have completed this, slowly bring yourself back to full waking consciousness and write down whatever information you received.

Method 2:

• Substitute the symbols for the colors in the above method. For example the key symbol for the 'Orange' university is a white owl or dog. You could imagine a dog is coming to you and leading you on a journey to find the answer to your problem.

CONCLUSIONS

These eight universities can be used in many practical and creative ways. They are an external source of help and knowledge that you can access through your mind. They are not located in any particular place or time, for they are outside the space/time continuum. In this sense they may also be considered a part of inner space, which we can enter through our imagination. All information is available to us and I don't believe there is a problem that confronts humanity that could not be solved by accessing these realms. They traverse time, and I think this is why some notable individuals like Leonardo da Vinci have been able to present ideas way ahead of their era. These abilities are available to all of us, not just a special few. It is important to remember that the information received will match the level of your own understanding.

When scientists collectively begin to open up these other dimensions, I believe that there will be a revolution in thinking that could transform this planet for everyone. These are exciting times: there is enormous potential for change to new ways of understanding and perception.

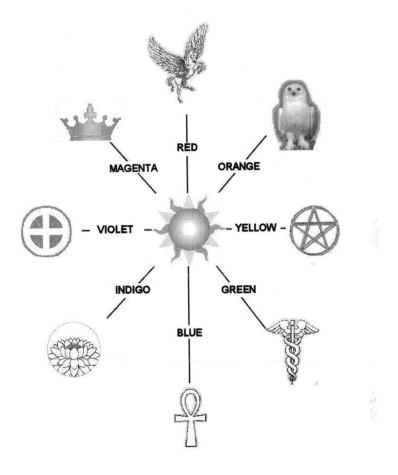

Fig. 5.3 Access symbols associated with the Quantum Universities, the spiritual centers of consciousness

Working with Your Dreams

Most people access higher dimensions of their being through their dreams. When we go to sleep, the conscious 'ego' control of the body is relaxed and our spiritual self is free to bring forward messages, from the unconscious that can help us understand and integrate the various outer experiences in our lives. As Carl Jung perceived those individuals and cultures that spend time processing their dream life are generally well-balanced people. Dreams speak to us in symbolic images that contain very precise messages. The Bible and other religious literature is full of stories on how dreams were used and interpreted to help understand some aspects of life. As I have discussed, visual images are frequently the way that the inner, spiritual self will communicate information to our conscious minds. Some people do not remember their dreams and believe that they rarely dream, but studies have shown that very few people do not dream at all. In most cases, for various reasons, I believe that individuals will block out messages from their dreams. With a little practice, this can be corrected. In this chapter, we will explore this important aspect of inner communication and the value that it can play in psi development.

THE MEANING OF DREAMS

The greatest difficulty that most people face in thinking about their dreams is the seemingly bizarre images that tumble over each other. Human beings have become used, particularly in western cultures, to communicating through the spoken word. Conveying information through symbols can appear alien to our conscious mind (perhaps less so now, as computers become more widely used). To understand how dreams work, let us suppose that you are in a country where no-one speaks your language. How would you communicate? The only way would be through gestures, drawings or showing pictures and pointing to objects. Eventually, someone would understand what you wished to convey, even if you were not successful at first. In a similar way, in dreams, the inner part of you is conveying messages to your conscious mind. It is true that language sometimes enters into the dream, when someone says something to you, but the most part of any dream will be symbolic.

Symbols act on the subliminal part of our mind, which is why advertisers work so extensively with them. Nowadays, most advertisements, particularly those on television, tend to use very few words: the advertisers have realized that images or pictures are a very potent way of conveying information that bypasses the logical parts of our mind. Logic is important, but it can also get in the way. Many people have had an intuitive hunch to do something that the logical part of their mind said was nonsense or impossible. However, acting on their intuition proved to be the correct solution to their problem. Advertisers believe that feeding your subconscious part with particular images will encourage you to act in certain ways, without fully realizing why you are doing so. In the same way, the inner part of you, through your dreams, will program information into the mind.

An important part of inner growth and development is learning to become consciously aware of the patterns and energies that weave through your life. Learning to interpret your dreams can be an important step in this process. This is not as difficult as it might seem. The first and most important thing to remember is that your dreams are messages that are being conveyed through dream symbols. All you need to do is learn to interpret the messages.

EMOTIONS IN DREAMS

The messages that come through from the deeper aspects of the self have to negotiate our feelings. Feelings are an important way of gathering information, but they can also cloud the issue. Think of those occasions where your emotional response to a person or situation caused you to make a rash judgment or action that you later regretted. In analyzing your dreams, you need to separate out your emotional responses to the images. For example, seeing yourself naked in front of a group of people may cause you to feel very embarrassed, either during the dream or afterwards when you think about it. But the image of nakedness is telling you something about yourself which the other images (where you were, who you were with) will elucidate. Methods for recording your dreams will be described later on, but it is important now to think about separating the images and the feelings.

TYPES OF DREAMS

Dreams fulfill a number of important functions, which will be conveyed through the type of dream. Dream researchers know that most people dream regularly several times a night but that we forget most of these dreams. It is usually only the dreams that come just before we awake that get retained. I think that our Higher Self is aware of this, which is why the most important messages are generally left to last. Dreams can be divided into a number of categories.

Sorting out: These dreams process the events of the previous day, sorting through your responses and making some order from your experiences. This process is rather like a computer storing information in its correct files and setting up all the necessary cross-references.

Instructional: Your higher mind, either through its own inner knowing or through its access to the 'quantum' highway, will convey information back to the conscious mind. These dreams will tell you about aspects of your life of which you are not completely conscious, and so warn you in advance. A dream about being robbed may indicate that someone is taking something from you in your everyday life. On a different level, some individuals feel that they receive much inner instruction during their dreams.

Problem-solving: We all wrestle with problems from time to time, whether on an emotional, physical or mental level. Through our ability to access 'quantum universities', the necessary knowledge to solve these problems is available. No problem is insoluble: there are always different solutions and often it is a question of determining which is the best.

Different challenges will come forward in our lives to help us develop and grow. Just as a teacher sets problems at school for the pupil to work upon, I believe that the highest part of your being will challenge you to explore different facets of life by confronting the problems that it throws up. Sometimes your dream mind will present very clear messages on how to solve a particular problem. Sometimes it will present options on the likely outcome if you follow a particular route.

To break out of a difficult situation often means confronting either our fears or the conventions of the society that we live in. Fortunately, many restrictive concepts, such as the attitude towards homosexuality, are changing so that society's perceptions are not such inhibitory factors. However, we can still be held back from acting in a certain way by what others may think of us: the attitudes of our parents can sometimes be very powerful inhibitors. Confronting fear is one of the biggest challenges that any individual has to face. You will never deal with fear by running away from it, only by meeting it head-on. I believe that your dream world will show you how you can do this.

Precognitive: The higher aspects of your being are not fettered by time or space and you will sometimes have dreams that indicate future events. These dreams will sometimes involve the collective psyche of humanity and you may occasionally get glimpses of the future that touch important human experiences. Those that stick in our minds often involve some tragedy, such as a plane crash or ship wreck. Psychic researchers discovered that many people had prophetic dreams about the sinking of the *Titanic*. Premonitions of this sort can have a personal implication in that they warn you about something, or they can be a result of accessing the human collective psyche.

Invasive: In my experience, when the control of our conscious mind is relaxed, the impressions from outside energies become more prominent. Sometimes, other individuals will have some form of hold over our psyches, for example when a parent obsessively dominates their grown offspring, or when an individual starts to exert control over their partner.

This invasive energy can be highlighted in dreams and is often responsible for the more frightening, nightmare dreams that most of us experience from time to time. Just being aware of the source of this invasive energy can be an important step in releasing this type of dominance. Working on your protections and learning how to de-link your energies will also help.

Visionary: Many Shamanic peoples seek higher guidance through their visionary experiences; these are either gained in a waking state or, more often, while dreaming. These dreams have a special quality about them that transcends normal experience. The power of the dream is such that the individual who experiences it cannot doubt that something important has happened. Such dreams will often set the tenor for the next phase of a person's life. This may require a complete change in their direction and lifestyle.

RECALLING YOUR DREAMS

Dream recall requires practice and patience. I suspect that there are a number of reasons why we forget our dreams: because we do not appreciate their importance, because of fear of what they might show us, or occasionally because of nightmarish dreams in childhood, which became too painful to recall consciously. In these cases, the mind gets into the habit of blocking out all dreams. Remember, even though you may not recall your dreams, you almost certainly will have them. So the problem is how to recall what you have experienced.

There is a thin boundary between being in the dream state, which is an altered level of consciousness, and being fully awake. Unless the dream is brought forward very quickly into the conscious mind, it will usually subside and be lost completely. Occasionally an incident later in the day will trigger a recall, but this should not be relied upon.

As the moment of waking is so crucial to remembering your dreams, you need to establish a method of recording them straight away. This can be done by keeping a dream diary and pencil by the bed, ready to jot down any impressions or key pictures, or with a tape recorder with the pause button set so that the tape can be started very quickly upon waking. One of the problems is that many people enjoy lying in bed and slowly bringing themselves around to full consciousness. When this happens, the dream images can easily be lost. However, with practice, it becomes possible to remember your dreams and still to allow yourself to wake up slowly.

If you do not remember your dreams, you will need to try to capture whatever fleeting impressions come forward at the moment of waking. This may at first just be a feeling or even a single image. Whatever it is, record what you have remembered. This has a way of moving the dream from the subconscious mind through to the conscious part of our self. It is an important step in the individuation process.

Once you have written down the dream in as much detail as you can, you will need to break it up into its different symbolic parts so that its message can be understood. Here is an example from my own dream world.

The Dream

I was driving my car to a place where I used to live, which was set on a hill. My younger son was with me in the car and when we stopped he jumped out and I got out quickly to chase after him. However, I left the brake off, and the car started to roll backwards down the hill and eventually crashed. In the dream I knew that this was an important message and that I had to remember the symbols and I kept asking myself, What does the car mean?' When I got to the car it was badly damaged and I said to myself 'The car's a write-off'. Then I woke up.

The best person to analyze your dreams is you; however, there are collective symbols that have a general interpretation. Sometimes sharing dreams will give additional insights so I give my interpretation below.

To obtain the message in the dream, you will need to break it down into individual pieces. To do this, draw up on a sheet of paper four columns as shown, using my dream as an example:

Symbol	ACTION	Feeling Response	Interpretation
child (son)	jumping out of car	apprehension	an aspect of the child within wanting to get out of a situation

When you do this, note any special features and any other meanings for the words in your dream.

The interpretation

The dream is set in a place where I used to live, so it represents some aspect of my past. In the dream, I am with my young son. Generally, all people who appear in dreams are aspects of us; in this case, he is the child within me. Children can represent the spontaneous parts of our being, or aspects of ourselves that have not grown up. In this case, the child within wished to get out of the car quickly. The car rolled down the hill which can either indicate going backwards in some aspect in life or reversing a situation.

Cars are fascinating symbols that have a number of layers to them. They are the vehicle that takes you through life, so they relate to some aspect of how you are conducting yourself. The dream mind can also work with puns, so thinking about other meanings for any particular symbol is important. I think the question, 'What does my car mean?' was a pun on the word karma. Karma is a Hindu word that is also a fundamental part of Buddhist philosophy. The nearest English equivalent is fate or destiny but karma also implies the consequences or results of actions carried out in the past, which can sometimes refer to past lives. In other words, if I am suffering some problem at the moment, it may be the consequence of some action or deed carried out in the past. All aspects of our lives are therefore seen as the result of karma, both beneficial (the good things that I have done) or detrimental (where I have harmed others). So, like our cars, our karma is an important vehicle which carries us through our life. In this case the car was a 'write-off' so an initial interpretation was that I was 'writing off' some karma. But here the pun came to the fore again, for, in order to reverse this karma, I actually needed to write off or send a letter to someone, which is what I had been contemplating in my waking state. The dream was giving me a message that this was the 'right' thing to do in order to 'write off' some karma. Certainly since following this dream message a change in dynamics has occurred.

In the dream, a number of puns or word plays appeared. You will often need to think carefully about the images in dreams to get the message. Sometimes, voicing the symbol out loud will indicate the meaning. These messages are very subtle and the obvious interpretation may not be the correct one. In my dream, I am sure that it was nothing to do with making certain that my brakes were on when parking my car on a hill.

INTERPRETING YOUR DREAMS

Many people find this difficult. It is true that, to begin with, it is very akin to learning a foreign language. The images of your dreams make little sense. With a little practice, you will soon learn what is being conveyed, for I believe that your inner mind wants to get its messages across and will do everything in its power to help. There are a few guidelines which can make a big difference in understanding how your dream mind works. These are drawn from many different dream interpretation books and my own working experience in this field.

SYMBOLS OR FACTUAL REALITY

There are two levels of reality when it comes to dreams. Are they presented in a symbolic way or factual way? These two modes are similar to those in any psi receptive experience. For example, if you dreamed about a close friend deceiving you, is the dream giving you a warning that this person is actually deceiving you, or is it telling you that part of yourself, symbolized by this person, is deceptive?

As a rule, it is always best to start by looking at all characters within the dream as parts of you. In the above case, I would encourage you to look at what is the deceptive part of you before suspecting your friend. Usually, other messages within the dream will make it clear which is which. To understand yourself in this context, write down all the things that you perceive about your friend. What is it that makes them attractive to you and in what way do they mirror you? This will sometimes give you the clue to the correct meaning of the dream. Remember, you cannot cheat yourself. Your inner motives will show up within your dreams and we all find aspects of ourselves uncomfortable. There is nothing wrong with this, as long as we tackle these parts of ourselves in a direct way. It is only when we avoid these issues that problems arise.

TIME AND PLACE

The next aspect of the dream that is important is its location in time and space. Is it in the past, present or future? This will give an indication of where the energy from the dream lies. Dreams about the past usually indicate aspects of our psyche that have not been properly integrated. It may be that as an individual you are living in the past. Dreams about the future may give information about future events.

The location of the dream is also important. Is it on familiar or unfamiliar territory? The latter will generally indicate aspects of yourself that are new to you. Buildings in dreams usually represent you. When on the top floor, you are in your mental or spiritual level; the ground floor or basement indicates the physical, sexual or subconscious parts of your psyche. Travelling on a lift or on the stairs represents the link between these parts.

Travelling in your dreams indicates your journey through some aspect of your life, sometimes showing you how you can get from A to B if there is a particular problem that needs solving. In these cases, carefully note the images at the start, middle and end of the journey, for they will give clues to the solution of your difficulty. Occasionally, such dreams indicate physical travel of some sort, but generally they refer to inner movement.

OTHER MAIN DREAM SYMBOLS

There are as many dream symbols in your inner world as in the outer. There are books that give general meanings which can be helpful but it is important to remember that it is your dream mind that is operating and therefore how you interpret your inner symbols will be unique. A few important general symbols are given here:

- **Water**
  Usually represents your emotions, although it can connect to the spiritual life force. Observe what happens when you come into contact with water. Are you in a boat, swimming in the sea, or drinking water? Each will give an indication of something that needs attention. Stormy seas, for example, indicate a difficult emotional period.

- **Fire**
  Less common than water and generally indicates either the creative, spiritual aspect of the self or anger. Note whether the fire seems under control or not.

- **Animals**
  Indicate the instinctive aspects of your psyche. Note carefully what the animal is doing and, when you come to interpret your dream, try to analyze what the animal means to you. A dog might symbolize faithfulness, a cat detachment, a hedgehog protection and so on.

- **People**
  Are generally aspects of your personality as they project out into the world. If you are frightened of people, this is related to those aspects of yourself that you fear. Occasionally, people in your dreams will relate to individuals in your outer life, but this is not the norm. Assess what the people are doing and how this relates to you.

- **Royalty**
  Relates to the higher aspect of yourself: your strengths, power and spiritual connections.

- **Flying**
  This can have a double meaning. Sometimes you will experience flying dreams where you act like Superman. This is how your psyche relays its perceptions of travelling 'out of your body" into other realms of consciousness. Flying in airplanes indicates your connection to the mental aspects of your being, the 'mind plane' (air plane) as opposed to the 'earth plane'. This can also indicate your link with the spiritual plane rather than the mental, so you will have to consider all the factors that surround the dream.

- **Colors**
  Have different meanings according to which color stands out. Dark colors usually indicate the shadowy aspects of the self, your fears or

doubts, while bright colors show positive traits or qualities. Think about your association with the color to assess its meaning. As a guide, the following are some of the traditional interpretations of the main colors:

Red: energy, anger, sexuality - (rage)

Orange: vitality, protection, inner seeking - (intransigence)

Yellow: clarity, mental activity, foresight - (cowardice)

Green: healing, balance, inner knowledge - (jealousy)

Blue: calmness, spiritual love, aspiration - (depression)

Indigo: peace, inner reflection, perception - (addiction)

Violet: vision, joy, intuition - (arrogance)

Magenta: wisdom, leadership, higher consciousness - (aloofness)

Pink: emotional love, peace, tranquility - (frivolity)

Gold: spiritual power, wisdom, protection - (greed)

Silver: sensitivity, quickness, reflection - (disdain)

White: purity, protection, inspiration - (concealment)

Black: wickedness, restriction, mourning - (spiritual challenge)

Grey: fear, despondency, sadness - (balance between extremes)

Brown: earthiness, conformity, financial ability - (frugality)

- **Numbers**

  Like colors, these convey precise information. There is a tradition that says all numbers should be reduced to a single digit, by adding each part together, to arrive at the correct interpretation. So, for example, if you dreamed that you were 15 years old six would be the key number (1 + 5 = 6). Numbers will be dealt with in the chapter on numerology.

- **Birth and Death**

  Contrary to what may be the obvious interpretation of these situations in dreams, death and birth represent important changes in your life, not physical death or birth. The latter indicates something new coming into your life. This might be a person, an idea, money or whatever. Death indicates the completion of something, which the dream will generally elucidate.

DREAM ON

The above ideas will give you an indication about how you can begin to interpret your own dreams. It might be helpful to acquire a book of dream symbols but remember that it is your dream mind that is conveying the message, drawing off your own inner connections. Always try to make your own assessment about the symbolism first, before consulting a guide.

SECTION 3

DEVELOPING PSYCHIC AWARENESS

CHAPTER 7

The Tools of the Trade: Methods of Psi Receptivity

There are two basic ways that you can work with the receptive aspects of your psi nature to gain insights and information about yourself and events. These are:

- **Internal communication**
  This works through your sensitivity to the various incoming psi messages. As we have discussed, you can 'pick up' information through one or more of four basic levels: kinesthetic, feeling, auditory or visual. By learning to interpret these levels, your range of available information is greatly expanded.

- **External communication**
  This works through the use of an external symbol or pattern that you observe or create, which then requires a further interpretation to obtain its message or meaning. Divination using Tarot cards is a good example of this approach. Specific cards are selected which then become the source of the information which the reader conveys. Intuition is still required to bring forward the correct insight for the particular person and situation, but the reliance on the inner self for the message is reduced. In these cases, the cards or other divinatory system act as a prop to the inner level of communication, giving a set of pegs to hang the intuition on. There are many different methods to this basic approach such as astrology, palmistry, numerology, cartomancy, graphology, runes, I Ching and so on. We will explore some of these in this section.

EFFECTIVENESS OF EACH SYSTEM

Both the above approaches have their strengths and weaknesses and no system is 'foolproof'. Internal communication can work extremely well if you have established clear channels to your inner wisdom. However, every psychic has their off days and this can be a problem if you are relying on being able to perform at specific times to earn an income.

When working on your own problems, you can decide on the most beneficial time to carry out your investigation. However, in these cases you have to be very wary of the desires of your own 'ego' getting in the way. Let us say that you have a very strong yearning to have a relationship with a particular person. The power of that need will generally override any other perception that suggests this might be inappropriate. Always be wary of strong 'ego' desires.

One of the problems that some novice psychics face when giving readings for others is simply feeding back the clients their own wishes or what they want to hear. It is very easy to confuse a true perception of the potential future from the wish fulfillments received from the mind of the person having the reading. Sadly some unscrupulous individuals play on these need desires of people to ensnare them into having many readings, often at great expense, which are generally quite bogus. If you need help at this level seek out an individual that has been recommended to you or go through a reputable organization.

The external methods, to an extent, avoid these problems in that the shuffling and laying out of the cards, I Ching or whatever, establishes a more objective pattern from which to make an assessment. The divinator would then have an extensive set of associations to call upon in making their interpretation. So, even if they were having an off day, this would not necessarily show up. The main problem with this method can be over-reliance on standard meanings, which may be off-target for the particular situation or individual seeking help. If you are carrying out a reading for yourself, you will again have to be wary of your 'ego' wishes. I have known many individuals who have received messages that to others are very obvious, yet have been misinterpreted because they do not wish to hear them.

In practice, being able to call upon a number of methods, both internal and external, is ideal, for this will give you the greatest array of possible information. In the first part of this section, we will focus on the internal methods of psi receptivity and in the latter part a number of tried and tested external systems will be explained.

SYNCHRONICITY

Skeptics will naturally question how a set of shuffled Tarot cards or the movement of the planets could give insights and information about a particular problem. This is a valid question, but unfortunately there is not a rational explanation. Carl Jung used the word 'synchronicity' to refer to those events which come together at a particular time to give a deeper meaning to a situation. Many people will have experienced 'coincidences' in their lives, without any suspicion that they served another purpose or were caused by some underlying, unconscious force. Perhaps the oldest of all the systems of external divination is that of I Ching, which was used in China at least 3000 years ago. Empirically, it has stood the test of time but defies western logic.

One explanation on how the selection of cards, astrological placements, I Ching hexagrams or whatever might give meaning to a situation is to suggest that the higher aspect of your consciousness is aware of the underlying trends and dynamics of your life. It then propels these patterns through all sorts of subtle means into your outer world; they then emerge as chance meetings, significant events and so on. Your Tarot reader, connecting to this higher aspect, will unconsciously select those cards that most neatly fit the situation. Certainly, people who have carried out readings for many years can attest to the uncanny way that the cards almost take on a mind of their own.

Clearly, if you cannot suspend disbelief in the possibility of such systems working, then it is better to rely on your own intuitional methods. At the end of the day, belief is very important.

CAN I FORESEE THE FUTURE?

Most forms of divinatory activity are aimed at giving insights into future events and the best courses of action to follow. Occasionally, individuals wish to know about past patterns and the trends that have led up to a set of events. This can help in re-evaluating the direction in one's life.

As we have seen, there is fluidity between the past, present and future. A good psi practitioner can perceive all the circumstances that are leading an individual in a set direction and may also be aware of the intent of the inner, spiritual, self of the enquirer. This will then give a good picture of what is likely to happen to them. However, free will can modify those trends, so the future is always open to change.

Clearly, when assessing the karma of large groups of people or the destiny of nations, those trends are more deeply set and will be much less open to wide variations. There are many prophecies at the moment relating to world upheavals, which suggest that momentous events will take place over the next few years. Although there is generally agreement among psychics that these changes will be enormous, some see them in destructive, cataclysmic terms and others see the birth of a new level of consciousness, leading to world peace. Both scenarios may be right, depending on which part of the globe you happen to reside in.

'MAKING' THE FUTURE HAPPEN

Another problem that confronts any individual who receives a reading is the potential to cause consciously whatever has been suggested. A few years ago, I came across a case of a woman who had been told by a psychic that she was going to marry an acquaintance who wore glasses. Because she implicitly believed in this pronouncement, she deliberately set out to track down everyone she knew who fitted this description, and eventually managed to persuade one of them to marry her. Various other events followed, until she began to realize that she was deliberately manipulating events to fit the readings. The simple rule is learn to discriminate and never accept blindly what you are told. A good psi practitioner will only ever give you guidance on possible futures and warn you of circumstances surrounding you which may cause problems. Above all, do not believe any pronouncements that fix the time of your death or that of someone close to you. It is a totally irresponsible act for any psi practitioner to make such suggestions, which, in my experience, are inevitably wrong. There are very powerful forces that prevent us seeing this aspect of our future unless there is some exceptional reason for this to be revealed, which only happens in very special circumstances.

PREPARATION

Before embarking upon any intuitive or psi receptive experience, you need to address your intention and make sure you are in the right frame of mind.

INTENTION

Intention is very important. You will need to decide in advance what questions you wish to ask and to frame them clearly in your mind. It can be helpful to write them down. There is a hierarchy of types of questions that will elicit helpful responses:

- Any question that helps you develop more fully as a person, providing this does not contravene the dictates of your spiritual self. Such a question can be, 'How can I better develop my musical talent?' The answer may come back that you need to change your music teacher or to go on a particular training course.
- Any question that aims to help you achieve better relationships with others. These could be friends, neighbors, parents, colleagues and so on.
- Any question that aims to give you better insight into helping another individual or individuals. There are a whole host of different situations that apply here: therapists seeking greater clarity in helping their clients; teachers wishing to help a particular pupil; lawyers concerned to give the best advice to their clients; or politicians wishing to give the best guidance to their country. Providing the intention is aimed at genuine help, and not coercion, and takes into account the real needs of the individual, there will be a positive response.
- Any question that aims to solve a particular problem in your life. This could be to do with health, money, personal growth or whatever. Such questions are very relevant at time of great changes. Knowing the best route to take can be very helpful.
- Any question that helps you develop the material aspects of your life, providing that this is not at the expense of others. Many business decisions fall into this category. In these situations, it is important that insight is sought into what is the greatest benefit that can be brought to all members of the team or company. Most companies at some stage or

another depend upon creative ideas or visions for their success and some, such as advertising consultants, need to generate new concepts all the time for their livelihood; indeed, it is perhaps vital that companies do so. The drive for excellence can be greatly assisted by insights from the 'quantum' realm.

Some questions will not get a positive or clear response. These include:

- Any question that tries to give you an upper hand over others in a way that might be detrimental to their well-being.
- Any question that aims to win money that has not been earned, such as gambling. (This is not to make any judgments about betting, but you cannot use the psi faculty to give yourself an unfair advantage over others in this way. There are protections built into this realm that ensure fairness for all.)

FORMING THE 'RIGHT' QUESTIONS

It is very important that all questions are presented to your higher consciousness in a way that allows a proper response to be given. There are a number of simple guidelines that apply to all systems of divination and these can be summarized as follows:

- **Simplicity:**
Frame all questions so that they can easily be answered. Do not ask double questions, such as, 'Should I take up this new job offer or stay in my present employment?' Instead, pose two or more questions: 'What would be the outcome if I take up this job offer?' and, 'What would be the outcome if I remain in my present employment for the time being?' You could also ask, 'Will a better job be offered to me within the next twelve months?' Such short questions will elicit a much clearer response than one long, confused question.

- **Specificity:**
Make sure that all your questions are aimed at precisely what you wish to know; whom you wish to know it about; when it will happen; and where it will take place.

- **Directness:**
Ask a clear question and you will get a clear answer. Ask a vague question and you will get a vague answer.

Warning: There can be a great temptation when asking questions to persevere, perhaps using different systems of divination, until you think you have received the answer that you wish to hear. You cannot con your higher consciousness in this way. What is important is for you to think deeply about the answer that you have received, even if you find it objectionable. If impediments are indicated, try to find out what these might be, rather than pretend they don't exist.

BEING IN THE RIGHT FRAME OF MIND

To receive the best responses to your questions, you will need to set up the right mental environment for this to happen. Science has shown how different brain rhythms reflect altered states of consciousness; inducing the right rhythm is important in encouraging psi activity.

Brain waves are measured in hertz, or cycles per second. Beta waves (13-26 hertz) are the normal, waking, conscious mode. Alpha waves (8-13 hertz) arise when the body is relaxed and the eyes are closed in meditation. These waves also occur when we day-dream with our eyes open. Theta waves (4-8 hertz) occur with deep relaxation, drowsiness, and dreaming sleep. Most people in this state do not maintain consciousness, but skilled meditators can reach this level and still be consciously aware. Delta waves (0.5-4 hertz) occur in deep sleep or unconsciousness.

The work of the late Max Cade in his book *The Awakened Mind* suggested that receptive psi activity takes place on the boundary between Alpha and Theta rhythms so for this to occur there needs to be a level of inner relaxation. To achieve this, carry out the exercise on the next page:

CREATING THE RIGHT SETTING

There can be many different locations where you may need to call upon your receptive psi abilities. However, when carrying out this work at home, it is preferable to establish a set routine and place for it. The mind tends to work better with regular patterns, and experience has shown that all psi activity will build up a vibratory atmosphere reflecting your work. This is why we can feel a sense of peace and calm in places where meditation is carried out regularly. This immediately makes it that bit easier when 'tuning in'. Think about your home and decide where the most appropriate place is to carry out your experimental work. You may like to burn incense or light a candle to create a more ambient environment.

Water is a helpful commodity to have around, and some people like to have a chalice or vase nearby containing spring water. Water is the most receptive of the elemental energies and draws to it inspirational qualities. Soft music can also help set up the right mood.

Whatever you feel helps create the right atmosphere for meditation will be conducive to psi activity. This has to be a personal preference and you can always experiment to see what helps. Once you have set up your location and carried out your preparation exercise, then you are ready to begin.

PSI RECEPTIVITY PRELIMINARY EXERCISE (time: 3 to 5 mins)

Aim: To induce a state of inner relaxation and alertness for psi activity

- Sit in one of the postures mentioned previously and close your eyes.
- Carry out the body awareness exercise in Chapter 2 and connect to your inner light.
- Surround yourself in your protective bubble of light.
- Think of the sun and imagine that there is a beam of light coming down to the top of your head, bringing forward the correct inspiration for the situation.
- Carry out your psi activity, whatever it is.
- When you have finished, de-link from the person or situation and from the sun and bring yourself back to full conscious reality.

RECEIVING THE REPLIES

Again, there are two ways in which you will receive responses to your questions. These are:

- Direct insight or communication to you through one of the psi receptivity levels.
- An obvious change in, or input into, some aspect of your physical world. This might take the form of someone making a suggestion out of the blue, saying something that immediately answers your question, or an unexpected job offer.

If you do not immediately get a clear response to your question through the first method, then keep an open ear for your reply to come through the second. If you do not appear to get any response from either of these two, re-frame your question. If you still do not get a response, you can always ask your psi faculty whether this is the right question to ask or what is blocking the response.

CHAPTER 8

Visual Images and Intuition

As we have seen, there are four ways that we can access information from the 'quantum realm':

- Body sensations or responses (kinesthetic) Clairsentience
- Feelings or gut reactions
- Auditory or linguistic input - Clairaudience
- Visual images (intuition) - Clairvoyance

During this and the following chapters, we will explore how you can develop each of these aspects of yourself.

INTUITION

Intuition is defined in the dictionary as 'an immediate insight or apprehension without reasoning'. I believe that this quality comes from the deepest layer of your consciousness where your spiritual self has accessed some aspect of the quantum realm and gained information about some event or situation. Sometimes, such information appears illogical but is later borne out by circumstances. Many great world leaders have displayed powerful intuitive qualities when they seem to have an uncanny ability to act appropriately in times of crisis: however, most of the time our intuition acts in less dramatic but still effective ways. We all have an intuitive ability which can give direction to our lives, connecting us to a higher level of guidance that can be enormously enriching. Perhaps the easiest way to draw forth your intuitional quality is through visual imagery.

VISUAL IMAGERY

Your visual perceptive faculty can act in two ways:

- By creating inner images that either have a symbolic meaning or are factually correct.
- By projecting images onto your outer world.

What does this mean in practice? In the first case, the images will appear in your mind as feeling pictures that you will then need to interpret. In the second, these images will occasionally seem to appear in your outer world. An example of this is 'seeing' a person's aura or some other psychic phenomenon such as an apparition - a ghost or vision of a holy person. Crystal gazers use this technique when looking into their crystal balls. These techniques can be classified under the headings of clairvoyance, metaphors and scrying.

CLAIRVOYANCE, METAPHORS AND SCRYING

CLAIRVOYANCE

The word 'clairvoyance' literally means 'clear seeing'. Psi information appears as coherent mental impressions which give insight into a particular problem or situation. Clairvoyance is really a free-flowing form of your normal visualization ability. Some people find it hard to visualize but with practice it can become easier. A simple visualization exercise was described in Chapter 4; here is a way to develop it.

VISUALIZATION EXERCISE (time: 3 to 5 mins)

Aim: To determine your visualization ability

- Sit in one of the postures described in Chapter 2.
- Carry out the body awareness exercise described in Chapter 2.
- Imagine that you are looking at the front entrance of your property and try to answer the following questions:
    'What type of door is it?'
    'What is the color of the door?'
    'What surrounds the door?'
    'What type of letterbox does it have?'
    'Where is the bell or door knocker?'
- When you have answered as many questions as you can, go and look at your door closely and see how accurate you were.
- Now take any household object such as a vase and put it on a table in front of you. Look at the vase closely for a few moments and then close your eyes and try to visualize the vase. Open your eyes and check your results.

Everybody's mind is different in terms of its ability to think either visually or linguistically. Our education tends to favor the latter but artists will usually have good visualization skills. With the above exercise most people would have some image of their door that although it had all the relevant details was not particularly clear. With practice, your imagining ability can be greatly improved, but the good news is that psi receptivity does not require a high level of visualization skill. If you knew the various features of your door from the pictures that came to your mind, then this is sufficient. You do not have to 'see' the door with absolute clarity. The important feature of clairvoyance is being able to be aware of these images and interpret them.

Your clairvoyant mind will work in a very similar way to your dream mind. In some senses they can be viewed as different aspects of the same function within you. As in dreams, your clairvoyant mind will sometimes throw up bizarre pictures. With dreams, the 'ego' consciousness is not available to block these out, but with clairvoyance it is. So, one of the biggest problems is having the courage not to dismiss what your mind is picking up. Many times in carrying out 'tuning in' exercises with my students, their inner self has presented the appropriate information, only for their 'ego' to doubt its validity and dismiss it. Indeed, I have done it myself when first starting to develop my skills. I was being given a sealed box to 'tune into' to assess what was inside and I saw an image of a Winged Scarab (beetle) from ancient Egypt. However, I could not believe that this was correct, so I made a vague fumbling response. When the box was opened, inside there was a winged scarab brooch. This experience taught me to trust what I picked up.

You will need to have the confidence to note down any pictures that you receive, no matter how 'wrong' they might appear, and not to block or dismiss them from your mind. Remember that this aspect of your consciousness is attempting to convey a message to you in picture form. It is not trying to trick you deliberately with irrelevant information. Your task is to pick up the picture accurately and then to interpret the message. Both take a little practice, but neither are in themselves intrinsically difficult.

In any clairvoyant exercise, you will need to be able to recall what you picked up. Some people like to talk into a microphone; others make notes on a pad. Adopt whatever method suits you best. When you have gathered as much as you can from the exercise, try to analyze the message given. To do this you can use all the methods given in the section on dreams.

Some people like to carry out these exercises in a group or with friends. This can be very effective as long as it is not taken too seriously. Sometimes, when you are put on the spot, it can give you a feeling of being back at school, causing you to block out any information that you might have had. A friend told me that when he attempted to carry out some simple clairvoyant exercises on a training course, he had got them all wrong. Yet when he tried the same exercises in another situation, when he could not care less whether they were right or wrong, every single answer he gave was correct. In other words, trying too hard to 'be right" blocked his answers. This is an important lesson to remember.

CLAIRVOYANT EXERCISES

There are many situations which are applicable to you when you start to develop your clairvoyant ability. Select one of the question areas from the previous chapter and write down your question clearly on a piece of paper. Think back to the quantum universities, one related to finding out information. A key animal code to this university is the symbol of a dog. To help you with your practice, we will use this code in the exercise.

CLAIRVOYANT EXERCISE (time: 5 to 10 mins)

Aim: To develop your clairvoyant skills

- Sit in one of the postures in Chapter 2 and close your eyes.
- Carry out the body awareness exercise described in Chapter 2 and surround yourself with your bubble of protection. Link to your inner light and that of the sun.
- Visualize a dog in whatever imaginary or real surroundings you like and try to see what sort of breed it is. Try to feel a connection with this inner messenger and ask it to help you bring forward the answer to your question.
- Think of the question and then allow your mind to be open and alert for any pictures that come to the surface. Note down all that appears.
- When you have finished, allow yourself a few moments to feel centered and balanced, and then bring yourself back to full waking consciousness.

You will now need to spend time thinking about what you picked up. To do this, it can be helpful to note down each item in the sequence in which it happened. For example, let us suppose that you have two job offers and do not know which one to take. You could ask your 'higher consciousness' what the consequences would be if you took job A and what they would be if you took job B.

Let us suppose that for job A, you had the visual image of a door that was firmly shut and for job B an airliner flying across the sea to another country. From these two images, job B would clearly appear to be the most promising, but there is further information available. Taking off in the airliner could be interpreted as reaching new heights in your career which will take you into a new position (the other country), but it might also indicate that the job itself will eventually involve a physical move to another country. If you are unsure about actually moving and wish to find out which interpretation is correct, you will have to ask further questions. If you are still unsure, there is a further exercise on how to ensure the best outcome for any situation which will be explained in Chapter 16.

With all these exercises, only practice will improve your skills. Carrying them out once or twice a week will go a long way to strengthening your psi receptivity. Do not be discouraged if at first you do not succeed. By combining exercises you will optimize your potential so that you will start to score more hits than misses.

METAPHORS

Metaphors are another form of the clairvoyant faculty but instead of allowing random images to appear, you work with a specific picture and use that as the main tool for the interpretation. One of the simplest metaphors is a door, which you can use for yes/no responses. Imagine a closed door in your mind and pose the question to the door, "If the answer to any question is 'yes' then the door will open; if 'no', the door will remain closed". This metaphor allows for some variation in that the door will sometimes open half-way, which will suggest that the question being asked is not specific enough, or that the answer may be either 'yes' or 'no', depending on circumstances not yet considered. Another metaphor would be to imagine, say, a wise owl to which you pose your question. If the answer is 'yes', the owl will nod its head; if 'no', it will shake its head; if you have not been specific enough, it will just blink at you.

There are hundreds of metaphors that you can use in this way, some more complex than others. For example, if you wished to 'tune into someone' to see whether they might be suitable for employment in your company, you could imagine them as a car and see what comes to mind. What sort of car is it? Does the driver appear to be in control? Are there any obvious faults on the car? Is the car alone or are there other cars with it? All these questions may provide you with information about the person. You might need to spend a little more time thinking about some aspects. Let us say that you were looking for a dynamic person for your company and you had short-listed two candidates. In 'tuning into' the first, you saw a sporty-looking car with a few dents and which appeared to be involved in an accident; the second was a more sedate saloon with no marks, and arrived safely at its destination. This would suggest that the first person was potentially the more dynamic but also more likely to be reckless. If you still felt that he or she was the most appropriate candidate, you would at least have some warning to keep a check on their activities.

This type of assessment can be applied in all sorts of situations where you require specific information on a subject. Where you are uncertain about information that you have picked up, you can always get friends who know this system to double-check it. I have often worked with others on a diagnosis of a situation with very positive outcomes.

One of the most useful metaphors for diagnosing the causes of disease in a person is a house (where the different floors relate to the layers of a person's being). In this metaphor, the basement relates to the subconscious or sexual aspect, the ground floor the physical, the first floor emotional, the second floor mental, and the top floor or attic the spiritual. For example, in 'tuning in' to a particular individual's problem, the image that came up was of a pleasant Victorian property, with the ground floor several steps up from the pavement. The ground floor rooms were being redecorated and there was a pipe leaking in the small kitchen at the rear. On the first floor, there was a person trussed up in the corner of one of the bedrooms and there were further leaks in the shower room. On the second floor, there was a man looking out of the windows using a telescope. The attic was only accessible by a ladder and contained a Buddha-like man who appeared to be meditating, but on further observation was seen to be sleeping. The basement was partly flooded by water from the kitchen and shower room.

This image is rich in symbolism and relates to a person with a number of recurring health problems. The raised ground floor suggests someone who is not properly earthed. The trussed figure in the bedroom suggests that something is being repressed at an emotional level; the figure on the second floor is looking in the wrong direction to sort out the problem. The character in the attic indicates a spiritual potential that is at present asleep. Water, the symbol of life force and emotional energy, is leaking away from the person and clogging up their subconscious mind (basement).

Discussing these images with the person in question proved helpful in highlighting the areas in their life which needed attention, leading to a great improvement in their health. It is important to appreciate that your health is dependent upon a balance being maintained between the physical, emotional, mental and spiritual aspects of your nature. If one of these levels gets out of balance, is neglected or repressed, it can manifest eventually as physical illnesses. You can carry out this type of visualization exercise on yourself by imagining that you are entering your own inner house and working with what you find there. You can even do this on behalf of another as in the case described. Many other metaphors can be used, such as a garden, tree, animal or castle.

METAPHORS IN THE OUTER WORLD

Shamanic practices suggest that we should also look for metaphors in the natural world around us, a concept which can be found in the idea of propitious or warning omens. One of the most dramatic instances of this type of event in my life occurred some years ago. I was walking up a path to attend a particular meeting which resulted in my dismissal from my job. I did not know that this was on the cards, but before I arrived, a snake came out of the wall on one side and crossed the path in front of me before going into some grass. (A snake in the grass?) Was this metaphor just a coincidence? I think not, judging by subsequent events.

Reading Tea Leaves or Clouds

Another way that symbolic images from the outer world can be used clairvoyantly is through tea leaf reading. When you have finished your tea, swill the cup three times and then upturn the remnants into the saucer. You will see some dregs on the bottom and sides of the cup. The idea is to allow your imagination to make associations with these patterns to arrive at an interpretation. If your mind can easily see patterns in everyday objects, you could have a lot of fun with this. I remember watching a cocky businessman asking a clairvoyant friend of mine at a party to read his tea leaves. When she looked into his cup her first comment was, "Who is the secretary that I can see sitting on your knee?" The man nearly died of embarrassment on the spot.

There are many different systems of divination which use similar techniques to interpret signs and patterns in the natural world. Some of these can descend into superstition, when an individual only acts when they have obtained the right sign or omen. Carried to extremes, this could mean that you spend the whole of your life in bed, frightened to venture into the outer world. Confronting difficulties is part of life and you cannot avoid them completely, no matter how hard you try. Clairvoyant perceptions and accessing the quantum realm for information will, however, add a new awareness to all that you do. It will also generally help avoid the worst mistakes and offer guidance when you meet some challenging problem.

Cautions & Warnings

This psi receptivity is suitable in situations in which the person using this method has a real, direct need for the information. You cannot use it just to pry into someone else's life for any devious purposes. If you do try to do something that is inappropriate, either deliberately or inadvertently, you will be blocked from getting the correct information. Therapists seeking to help their clients will get many insights using this system, but you will still only be allowed to see what is appropriate for the particular situation or circumstance.

There is one group of people who you should not try to 'tune into'. Do not, under any circumstances, try to diagnose or assess any seriously disturbed individual. Therapists using any of these methods to gain insights into their patients should only do this on individuals that are known to them and not before someone comes to them for help. The chaotic energies around mentally disturbed people can sometimes be very strong and require specialist treatment. Apply these ideas and systems to situations that arise naturally in your life and you will have no problems.

METAPHOR EXERCISES

The exercise on the next page uses a metaphor to gain some insight into yourself.

Carrying out these exercises will present you with powerful insights into how you relate to different qualities. It is important to remember that your inner and outer worlds reflect each other: although an animal is something from the outer world, it also has an inner meaning within your psyche. Working with many hundreds of people has shown me that the more unexpected the color, animal or item of clothing, the more that you are in touch with the deeper layers of your consciousness, because in these cases rational perception is not obstructive. It is therefore important to try to bypass the logical part of your mind in these exercises. For example, let us say that you wished to consider the quality of power or strength. The logical part of your mind might associate this quality with a lion but, if in doing the exercise a mouse came forward, this clearly would not be an image produced by your logical mind. You will then need to reflect on the strengths of a mouse and where its power lies. When individuals are looking for an animal to symbolize protection they will sometimes imagine a deer or similar creature. This image is telling them that, like a deer, their best protection is to be sensitive to what is going on, and to take flight at the sign of any trouble, rather than by staying to fight.

Try always to accept the first image that appears and do not reject it. This will sometimes require courage to face aspects of yourself with which you are uncomfortable. We all have them, and confronting your inner fears or dislikes about yourself is an important part of the hero/ heroine's quest.

Once you have established an image for your relationship, you can go back and change the dynamic of this contact. For example, you could try to build up a better relationship with the badger in your imagination. Ask your higher consciousness such questions as, 'How can I become its friend?'

In the same way, whenever you wish to access that quality in your life, imagine the color, animal and item of clothing being with you. This will draw the corresponding energies to you and make an enormous difference in the way that you interact with other people.

Metaphor Exercise (time: 5 to 10 mins)

Aim: To develop your clairvoyant skills and gain inner perception

- Decide on a question that you would like to access within yourself, such as love, peace, integrity, joy, firmness or nourishment.
- Sit in one of the postures in Chapter 2 and close your eyes.
- Carry out the body awareness exercise in Chapter 2 and surround yourself with your bubble of protection. Link to your own inner light and that of the sun.
- Suppose that you wish to access your relationship with peace. Ask yourself the following questions and note the images that come to mind:

    What color do I associate with peace?

    Where would I locate this color in my body?

    What animal would I associate with peace?

    What is this animal doing? How is it relating to me? Do I feel comfortable in its presence?

    What item of clothing would I associate with peace? How do I feel when I wear that item of clothing?
- When you have completed these questions, bring yourself back to full waking consciousness and write down your responses.
- Think about what came to mind and try to assess how this relates to you. For example, if the animal that came forward was a badger which did not seem very friendly, you will need to ask yourself honestly in what way you are finding it difficult to relate to the quality of peace.
- Analyze and reflect on all the symbols that you picked up in this way.

Scrying

Scrying is based on the projection of your inner images onto a physical object, which could be a crystal bowl, bowl of water, mirror or some other reflective surface. There are many accounts of this ability in legend and fairy tales: Snow White's stepmother uses a magic mirror to discover who is the fairest in the land.

The simplest way to begin to see whether you have any scrying skills is to try the following exercise.

SCYING EXERCISE (time: 5 to 10 mins)

Aim: *To develop your clairvoyant skills and gain inner perception*

You will need a plain-colored, preferably white bowl, filled about half full with water.

- Sit somewhere with subdued lighting and a plain ceiling as this will be reflected in the bowl. The trick to make this type of imagery work is to put your mind in a relaxed, trance-like state – aware, but not controlling any images.
- Carry out the body awareness exercise in Chapter 2 and surround yourself with your bubble of protection. Link to your own inner light and that of the sun and connect in your mind to the symbol of a lotus flower. This will give you access to the right quantum level university.
- Look into the surface of the water and allow your mind to be open to any images that start to appear. With some people, this happens very quickly; with others, it takes a little time.
- Note the images that occur and try to interpret them afterwards in exactly the same way that you would for dreams. Successful scryers eventually get to know their images and can quickly interpret them.
- When you feel that you have obtained as much information as you can, bring yourself back to full waking consciousness and spend a moment balancing your energies.

You can do this exercise with friends, trying to open up so that you can help with their problems. Remember, like dreams, these images are usually symbolic so if you see any pictures of death or accidents do not assume that this means actual death or physical injury. In the symbolic world, death indicates a change from one state to another. Also, as long as your intention is to help, you will never 'pick up' anything that is inappropriate or harmful to another.

This exercise can be adapted and used with other tools such as a crystal ball, mirror or other reflective surface. The procedure should still be the same and practice will show you whether you need any additional props, such as music, to aid your relaxation.

'SEEING' AURAS

The best way to see an aura is to look at the person sitting against a plain, preferably light, background. Unfortunately, you will have to stare at them, so it is not generally appropriate behavior with someone you do not know. However, there might be occasions, such as a lecture, where you can subject the speaker to this type of scrutiny without causing offence. Alternatively, you can try out this exercise with any friend or colleague who is willing to be a guinea pig.

Get the person to sit in a chair with their back to the wall. You will need to sit opposite them, six to ten feet away. Slightly squinting your eyes, look at the wall beyond their head and see whether you can perceive a 'halo' effect around their head. Many people will initially dismiss what they perceive as a trick of their eyes or of the light, but, with practice, this 'halo' will start to grow and you may then begin to 'see' colors within it. Often, the aura will appear to be stronger on one side than the other. If you perceive this, ask the person whether they have had any aches, pains or accidents involving the side of the body with a weak aura. It has been my experience that a weak aura on one side reflects a problem of this sort.

AURAS OF ANIMALS AND TREES

All living things have an aura which is indicative of the life force running through them. If you are short of human beings to practice on, you can always look at your pets, plants or any trees that you happen to come across. You will be convinced that this is not all wild imagination when you begin to detect differences between the auras of the things you are looking at. I will sometimes get a few people to sit near each other against a plain wall and then have a number of people looking at the differences in their auras. It is amazing how distinct they all are and how easy it is for people to distinguish this.

FINALLY

All these clairvoyant exercises are designed to help you unlock your intuitive mind. Like a rusty machine, it sometimes needs a little oiling, and occasionally side effects such as headaches occur. Do not be alarmed if this happens. Sit quietly, re-balance your energies, and if this does not work you can always take an aspirin.

CHAPTER 9

Auditory and Feeling Responses

The next two methods of psi receptivity relate to auditory messages or clairaudience, automatic writing and your feeling responses, which are often called 'gut' reactions.

CLAIRAUDIENCE

'Hearing voices' in your head can be a disturbing experience, but it is generally an aspect of the psi function. Many people have, at some stage in their life, had the feeling that some important message is being spoken to them. Speaking is our normal means of communication and one might ask why our psi function uses other systems instead. I think that there are two answers to this question. Firstly, the powerful link of language to rational thought modes makes it difficult for our 'intuitive' mind to get its messages across. If you hear a voice inside your head communicating something that does not immediately make sense, you are likely to dismiss the message out of hand. Secondly, the very commonplaceness of language relegates it to the realm of normal physical experience. It is often easier for the deeper layers of your consciousness to communicate by other methods.

However, some people find that inner auditory messages are a very powerful source of insight and wisdom. Socrates was guided throughout his life by a voice that told him what to do. St. Joan was similarly assisted, and the English poet William Cowper claimed that he heard voices giving him advance notice of all the important events in his life. These messages usually take the form of a voice speaking inside your head, sometimes as though it was on a telephone line. You pose the question and an answer comes back straight away. It sometimes takes a little practice to 'hear' these messages, but they are not difficult to pick up. Very occasionally, they can be received as an audible voice but this is not normal.

WHERE DO THE VOICES COME FROM?

All inner voices are monitored and translated through your higher consciousness, so in one sense they arise within you. However, the original source of the information may be outside your consciousness. Let us say that you require information on a certain subject. You inwardly dial up the correct code, and someone who has the answer relays that information back to you in a linguistic form, which your mind then relays as an inner voice: all quite normal and natural.

As with the internet, there are a few potential problems with this system, but also many benefits. Firstly, you need to be sure that you have made the right inner connections and your question has been framed in a clear way. Confused questions provide confused answers. Secondly, it is very important to judge any response in the light of your own inner sensibility. Let us suppose that you dialed an open request for information on a particular subject that could be picked up by anybody: you may get a reply from someone who knows much less about the subject than you do. The answer here is to make sure that you are posting your enquiries through to the 'quantum' university network, so that you ensure a much higher level of insight and wisdom in the replies that you receive. The key codes to this network are described in Chapter 5. Even so, you will still need to ponder on any replies with your own conscience. It is ludicrous to carry out some act just because a voice inside your head tells you to do something.

CLAIRAUDIENT EXERCISE (time: 10 mins)

Aim: To develop your clairaudient skills

- Sit in one of the postures in Chapter 2 and close your eyes.
- Carry out the body awareness exercise in Chapter 2 and surround yourself with your bubble of protection. Link to your own inner light.
- Think of a sun disk and imagine that you are linking yourself to this symbol through a golden thread of light which will act rather like a telephone line. The sun is a symbol of your higher consciousness and will also link you through to one of the quantum universities.
- If you have a question, ask it in your mind to the sun and await a reply. You should start to hear a voice speaking to you. If you have no specific question, just opening up to higher wisdom will often produce a response.
- When you have finished, disconnect, close down and make sure that you ground yourself properly.
- Write down what you picked up to check, verify or keep for reference.

There are many benefits to this form of communication. The answers given are in a form that can generally be understood and they can carry a wide range of different types of message. Information is sometimes given in great detail, providing many insights into different aspects of life in a way that is readily accessible to most people.

To ensure that you make the right inner connections, I have described a precise method of working, to which you should adhere.

WARNINGS

Part of the traditional initiatory process for those exploring the spiritual world involves learning discrimination. You need to determine what is appropriate for you and what is not. In this context, there are three types of message which you should be on your guard against; these are:

- **Ego inflationary**: any message that suggests that you or the group that you are connected with has been specially selected for some important purpose or divine mission. Everybody is special and every life is important, no matter how humble it may appear. Into this category also comes any intimation that you had some exulted past life as a known historical character. Although I believe it is just possible that some important spiritual teachers are back in incarnation, the odds against you being one of them are very much greater than you ever winning the national lottery. Moreover in this case, such information would be blocked from the conscious mind until you had reached an advanced level on the initiatory journey. This takes many years. So, it is much better for you to work on the basis that you are a normal soul treading your own path of spiritual growth.

- **Fear inducing**: any message that tries to induce fear if you do not abide by what is said is suspect. Any true spiritual message is always offered in the context of you having the free will to accept or reject what is being said, without strings. Always be on your guard if any quality of fear underlies a message such as, 'If you do not believe this, something terrible will happen to you.'

- **Inhibiting free will**: any message that tells you that you must not believe or think about certain issues should be challenged. Free will is the gift of every soul, and although laws have been established to ensure the smooth running of society, the only important spiritual law that is really relevant can be summed up by Christ's words, 'Do unto others as you would have them do unto you.' You have no right to impose your will on others and you should pay no heed to any message that encourages intolerance of others.

These three yardsticks can be used to determine the underlying quality of any 'spiritual' message or teaching that you come across. Many new cults and groups are emerging at the moment. If you ask yourself,

'How do their teachings stand up to the above criteria?' you will not go far wrong in assessing their true spiritual worth.

AUTOMATIC WRITING

This is really another aspect of the auditory response, but in this case the information is channeled directly through the arm and pencil onto a pad of paper. Those who use this technique are able to block out their conscious control and access their higher mind directly through their subconscious. Messages are then written down without any thought interference, as though someone else is writing the message. As with all aspects of psi receptivity, your consciousness may well have been accessing information on the quantum highway and the information may feel as though it was coming from an outside source. However, it will have been monitored and relayed by your 'higher' self.

Automatic writing is often a way into exploring your inner world. It is important that you adopt the same procedures as those given above for clairaudient messages.

AUTOMATIC WRITING EXERCISE (time: 10 mins)

Aim: To develop your automatic writing skills

You will require a pad and pencil.
- Sit in one of the postures in Chapter 2 and close your eyes.
- Carry out the body awareness exercise in Chapter 2 and surround yourself with your bubble of protection. Look to your own inner light.
- Think of a sun disk and imagine that you are linking yourself to this symbol through a golden thread of light which will act rather like a telephone line.
- Open your eyes and write down whatever comes through to your mind without trying to block, censor or analyze the messages. Do not worry if complete nonsense emerges initially; if you practice, messages will start to come through that have some meaning.
- When you have extracted a message, read it carefully, trying to understand how it may be relevant to you.

You will need to look at what you have written down with a critical eye, bearing in mind the warnings discussed above. However, do not be discouraged if your initial attempts do not seem to bring forth any meaning. As with all aspects of this work, patience and practice will pay dividends. Automatic writing is not for everyone, but those who have found it has worked for them have been well rewarded.

YOUR FEELING SENSES

This can be one of the hardest areas to work on. It is not that we do not feel, but it is often very difficult to put a word to the underlying emotion. To understand this aspect of our being, we normally use language to describe the various emotional experiences. Language is a tool of the mind, not of the emotions, so we already have to make inner translations in how we describe what we are feeling. Moreover, many people are out of touch with many aspects of their feeling self and this makes it difficult to assess what they are picking up. However, emotions and feelings are an aspect of your consciousness and can be a very valuable way of assessing what you are picking up. It is a good little exercise, when confronted by any problem, to ask yourself both what you think about it and what you feel about it. When you connect to your feeling self in this way, try and put a word to that feeling. For example, consider your daily work, whatever it is. Ask yourself what you feel about this job. Do I feel bored, happy, excited, depressed, angry or apprehensive? As you read this book, you can also ask yourself what your feelings are at the moment. With a little practice, you will begin to be able to assess objectively what it is that you are feeling.

FEELING VERSUS THOUGHT

At a psychological level, the feeling self is very potent. It does not matter if the logical part of your mind tells you that what you are feeling is stupid; what you are feeling will dominate your consciousness. Phobias of all types may be illogical but they hold individuals in their grip. It is not quite true that, in a tussle between thinking and feeling, the emotional side wins hands down each time, but it is very important to honor your emotional self and not reject what your feelings are telling you. This does not mean that you have to give in to your feelings and act them out, but you do have to own them. If I felt very angry with someone I might feel like hitting them on the nose, but this would hardly be an appropriate way to act. However, denying what I am feeling starts to cut me off from my feeling self.

FEELINGS AND PSI RECEPTIVITY

Feelings or gut reactions are a very valid way of accessing your psi receptivity. They can be very accurate in giving you insights into problems or situations that the logical part of your mind will miss. It is important to separate these feeling responses from the kinesthetic perception which comes about when we listen to the messages from the physical body. The emotions and the body are closely linked, which is why you have bodily sensations such as being choked with anger when strong emotions flow through you. However, the emotions or feelings are an energy band in themselves, and I am sure that you will have been, at some stage of your life, in a situation where you have felt a strong emotional energy coming from an individual. This can often happen in meetings, where undercurrents of feeling are being expressed emotionally but not verbally. A typical situation would be where someone makes a statement that your feeling self immediately tells you is incorrect. If your feeling self is saying one thing, but your logical mind another, listen to your feelings; they will rarely let you down in this context. This is what gut reactions are all about. All parts of you are important and each aspect has an important job to fulfill in the expression of who and what you are.

With practice, you can learn to listen to these emotional feeling responses to perceive other layers of meaning and insight in any particular situation. Psychologists, psychotherapists and counselors in particular need to use this aspect of their receptivity to pick up the subtle shifts of energy that a person is expressing while they relate their problems. The following exercise will help the development of this aspect of your psi receptivity.

FEELING EXERCISE (time: 5 to 10 mins)

Aim: To develop your feeling self

- Think of the names of six people that you know reasonably well and write them down on a piece of paper.
- Sit in one of the postures in Chapter 2 and close your eyes.
- Carry out the body awareness exercise in Chapter 2 and surround yourself with your bubble of protection. Link to your own inner light.
- Take each name in turn and try to connect to them at a feeling level by asking yourself what feelings you are getting from them?
- Note down the responses in each case and when you have finished think about what you picked up. Were there any surprises?

If you practice this exercise you will soon get to distinguish the different feelings that you receive from people. In this context, it can be an extremely useful diagnostic tool.

Both our auditory and our feeling senses are important ways of accessing the quantum realm and picking up information when we are with other people. It will take time to develop these two aspects of your psyche, but the effort will be worthwhile.

CHAPTER 10

Dowsing and Kinesiology

The fourth way that you can pick up psi information is through the responses of your physical body. These manifest themselves as sensations in the skin or muscles and are a separate phenomenon from the feeling responses discussed in Chapter 9. Many trainee healers, when giving healing for the first time, comment on the tingling or warmth that they feel in their hands. This is caused by the flow of healing energy and is a commonplace phenomenon with experienced healers. Recipients too will often experience similar sensations, especially if the healing is being focused to a specific place in the body.

Such sensations are a normal part of the psi function and they have been harnessed in different ways in the past to access our extra-sensory perception. The most common method is through dowsing, but in recent years considerable progress has been made in health diagnosis using kinesiology or muscle testing. Both these systems will be explored in this chapter.

DOWSING

The concept behind dowsing is very simple: it is based upon minute movements or twitching occurring in the muscles in response to external psi activity. It does not matter what level this information comes to us from, as resonance will translate its energy through to every other level, including the physical body. The effect on the physical body differs from person to person but generally it will produce slight movements in the muscles which, if amplified, can become a reliable diagnostic tool. In times past dowsers, particularly when looking for water, would use a 'Y'-shaped hazel rod, but nowadays there are a host of different implements that can be used, from pendulums to bent coat-hangers and strips of plastic. These systems tend to work on a simple yes/no response level, where the movement in the divining rod or pendulum changes when the required response is felt or located.

There is evidence that forms of dowsing were used in ancient times. One of the most common uses of this system in the past was in the search for water, but before geological surveys were available, dowsing was also used effectively in locating mineral deposits. There are also old records of divining rods being used to find missing people, and to track down criminals. Its predominant use today is directed to health issues, such as determining which substances may cause allergic reactions, Radionic healing and the causes of health imbalances. Before you can start exploring this facet of your psi make-up, you will need to make or acquire some dowsing tools.

There are three main types of divining implements: pendulum, divining rods and forked sticks. The latter are usually replaced nowadays by plastic strips. It does not matter what material the objects are made of, for they are only magnifying your body's reactions. They are not picking up information themselves. It used to be thought that with water divining, some subtle energy from the flow of water affected the hazel rod, causing it to bend up or down. Rods made of hazel and no other substance had to be used because of its special affinity with water. We now know that this is not true. Any material can be used, for it is the body that is responding and all the rods are doing is magnifying this altered state.

PENDULUMS AND THEIR USES

A pendulum can be any weighted object suspended from a piece of fine string that allows it to swing or gyrate easily. They come in all shapes and sizes and can be purchased from New Age shops. If you do not feel like spending any money you can always make your own. A very simple form of do-it-yourself pendulum is a Yale key suspended from a 250 mm length of cotton yarn; alternatively, you could use a ring or metal washer as the weight. Shop-purchased pendulums usually take the form of a carved wooden, crystal or metal plumb bob suspended from a fine piece of thread. Whatever you adopt, you will need to be comfortable with the balance of the pendulum. If you decide to purchase a ready-made pendulum, ask to try out several to find out which 'feels' right.

Once you have made or acquired your pendulum, you can have fun experimenting with it. Don't take things too seriously to begin with and expect to get all your answers correct. It takes a little time and patience to build up confidence in its use. Pendulums basically work on a yes/no response although, as we shall see, there are some variations that can be added.

To use a pendulum, hold the thread between your thumb and first finger approximately 150 mm to 225 mm (6" to 9") from the bob and set it swinging in a backwards and forwards motion. One of the simplest diagnostic methods is to think of a question which has a yes/no answer and then wait to see whether the pendulum starts to gyrate clockwise or anti-clockwise, having first determined which direction would be yes and which no. You can do this simply by asking inwardly beforehand: 'Show me which way is yes', then waiting to see which way the pendulum moves. Several variations of this method can be used, such as backwards/forwards movement being yes and a gyrating movement no.

The biggest problem, as with all psi receptive methods, is the interference from the conscious mind. As soon as you believe the answer to any question is either yes or no, you will interfere with the pendulum's response. It is very important that you put your mind into a passive state when carrying out any diagnostic exercise, so that you are asking your body to give the reply, not your rational mind. Good dowsers are able to do this, to listen to what their body is saying', but it does take regular practice and you shouldn't be put off if, to begin with, you get the wrong answers.

PROTRACTOR METHOD

The system that I have found the most effective and easy to use is the protractor method. You will need to draw a semicircle on a sheet of paper and divide it into two equal quadrants (Figure 10.1). Instead of gyrating, in this method, the pendulum will give the answer by swinging towards one side or the other. The advantage of this system is that it allows for variations in the yes/no response. Swinging completely to one side or the other is a very definite yes or no; staying close to middle is a more qualified response and may take more questions for the answer to become really clear.

To follow this method, you may need to shorten your grip on the thread to between 50 to 75 mm (2" to 3"). Ask within yourself which side will be yes and set the pendulum in a backwards/forwards motion along the centre line of the quadrant (see Fig. 10.1). Watch which side it starts to move towards and mark this down with the letter Y. Now pose your question and start the pendulum moving once again; which side it moves to will indicate whether the answer is yes or no. To test yourself using this system, select a dozen cards at random from a deck of playing cards, shuffle them and lay them face down beside you. Ask the pendulum to indicate which side is black and which is red. Then taking each card in turn, ask the pendulum to tell you the sequence of colors of the cards. Wait until you have finished before checking.

With a little practice, you should start to score above 50% regularly; however, three things can get in the way of this type of exercise. The first is confidence, or the lack of it. Belief in the effectiveness of any method using your psi nature is paramount. As soon as you start to doubt your abilities you set up a negative response, which can then become self-defeating. You will need to get over this problem and one way that scientific testers try to do this is by repeating their successful experiments. As with many walks of life, the more successful you are, the more successful you are likely to become.

Secondly, testing with playing cards, although excellent because of its random nature, has no real intrinsic value. For this reason, your psyche may opt out from this type of experiment. Thirdly, being put on test, where the answer has to be either right or wrong, brings up many memories from school exams which can cause further complications.

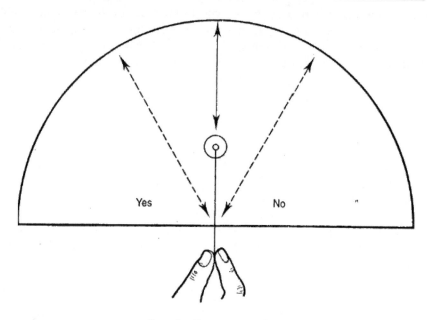

Fig. 10.1 Protractor method

At quite a deep level, none of us likes to be wrong and this can become a psychological barrier to this type of approach. Even experienced dowsers are not infallible, so do not be discouraged if it takes a little time to master these techniques.

EXPANDING THE PROTRACTOR METHOD

Once you have started to use this method, it can be applied in all sorts of situations. For example, you could test yourself for food sensitivities, which many people find problematic. You could ask the following questions:

- Do I ever suffer from food intolerant reactions? Yes/No?
- Are these reactions sporadic or regular? Yes/No?
- If sporadic, do they happen at set times in the month? Yes/No?
- If regular, which foods or substances am I allergic to? (Write down a list and go through each item in turn.)

When you have completed your list, experiment with removing these items from your diet or environment and see what happens to your health and vitality. This type of exercise will not cause any harm, as long as it is not overdone, and may do a lot of good. It also removes any pressure which the card exercise might induce.

Warning: if you find that there appear to be many foods that are giving reactions, you must get this checked by a specialist. It is not recommended that you radically alter your diet without first consulting a nutritionist. If your responses suggest that you cut out sugar, wheat or coffee, then this will not cause any harm, at least in the short term. Variations in diet can be beneficial and you should always be able to tell how well your body is responding by the state of your health. But if in any doubt check with a suitably qualified therapist or doctor. The protractor method can also be used in situations where some form of calibration is required. For example, let us say that you have used this method to determine which Bach flower remedies you need to take. It may be necessary to take them as a regular dose every so many hours. If you have calibrated your protractor with numbers you can ask the pendulum to indicate the correct time sequence and get an immediate response. This can save a little time, although all questions of this sort can be broken down into yes/no answers, for example, 'Should I take this remedy every hour? Yes/No?' and so on.

Map Dowsing

Another main use for the pendulum is map dowsing. This can be used to discover missing persons, different 'ley' or earth energies, underground springs, mineral deposits and so on. In these cases, your higher mind accesses the quantum realm and relays the information gathered. The map acts as a focus for that information. Map dowsers use different techniques to gather their information, such as pointing to certain areas on the map and asking yes/no questions. The method I normally use for determining the centers of chaotic or positive psi energy that might influence the residents of a house is to set the pendulum in motion along the bottom left-hand corner of the map and mark down the line of the angle that the pendulum makes (if any) onto the map. Then I move to the bottom right-hand corner and do the same thing. I then extend the two lines until they cross. Before completing this, and to double-check, I will normally turn the map at right angles, cover the centre so that I am not being unduly influenced, and repeat this process so that I end up with four lines. Because it is difficult to be completely accurate in noting down the exact alignment of the swings of the pendulum, these four lines do not always exactly coincide, but they do give a general position that can then be refined by further checking. I am sure that in times to come the police will start to use these systems to track down criminals and to discover the whereabouts of missing people. Ideally, these methods need to be set up in a proper unit within the police force using people who have been trained in these techniques. By incorporating the best of both scientific and psychic investigation, a much higher level of successful detective work would be achieved.

> DOWSING EXERCISE (time: 15 to 20 mins)
>
> ### *Aim: To teach the rudiments of dowsing*
>
> - Spend a few minutes relaxing yourself, connecting to your inner light before starting to dowse. This will ensure that your responses will be coming from the highest part of your consciousness.
> - You can pose any question to the pendulum for its reply. However, you must make sure that you put yourself into a meditative state and try to keep the rational side of your mind at bay. It is always a good idea to avoid questions that carry an emotional response for you. If you ask, 'Will I win the lottery?', your desire could override a proper answer.
> - For this exercise, ask about substances that may cause allergic reactions on the basis of the questions above.
> - When you have noted down the answers, see how they appear to fit. You might like to think up other questions that can expand on this diagnosis.
> - Repeat this test a few days later and see whether you pick up the same results. You could also use this method to test out the members of your family.
> - One word of warning. Always check when you start each session which side is yes and which is no also women will often find a switch in polarities during their menstrual cycles or when pregnant. Sometimes quirky situations happen, for no apparent reason, creating a switch in the polarity of one's psyche. This, in turn, can cause a reversal in the way that the pendulum moves.

FINDING LOST OBJECTS

Another practical use for your pendulum is finding lost objects. This can be done using a combination of the yes/no response method and the map dowsing method. Let us assume that you have lost a ring and do not know whether it is in your house. The first question you can ask is, 'Is the ring in my home?' If the answer is yes, then draw a sketch of your house and using the map dowsing method assess the location of the ring. Alternatively, by inwardly asking a series of simple questions such as, 'Is the ring on the ground floor?', Is the ring in the kitchen?' and so on, you will eventually narrow down its position. If you are wrong at first, try again until you are successful.

DIVINING RODS

In the past, a single, fairly long, straight rod or wand was used, but today it is more usual to use bent rods. These are often no more than adapted wire coat-hangers. If you are using coat-hangers, cut them using pliers as indicated in Figure 10.2 and bend the short and long arm at right angles to each other. The rods are held loosely in clenched fists, with your elbows tucked in close to your sides. They should point away from your body at chest height and be parallel to each other, like a pair of pistols.

In order to get the 'feel' of movement of the rods, slightly turn your wrists inwards and you will notice that the rods move immediately together, probably crossing over each other. Now turn both wrists outwards and this time the rods will separate, pointing away from each other. Next turn your wrists together, the left outwards and the right inwards - both the rods will point to the left of your body. When you turn your wrists in the opposite direction, the rods will point to the right. You therefore have four directions that you can use: crossing over, moving apart, turning to the left or turning to the right. These four directions can be used for divining. A diviner will walk slowly over a piece of ground, holding the thought of what it is that they are seeking, and watching for when their rods move through the slight muscle responses of arms and wrist.

THE USES OF DIVINING RODS

Rods come into their own in all outdoor locations. They have an advantage over the pendulum in that they are not affected by windy conditions. Rods are effective in locating underground water, drains, broken water pipes, cables, 'earth' energies, archaeological objects and so on. If you go to sites such as Avebury or Glastonbury, you will often see dowsers with their rods walking over the ground looking for energy alignments.

THE ROD METHOD

Let us assume that you wish to locate a damaged field drain that runs across a particular piece of land but whose position is unknown. First, find a known drain run and, using the method described above, walk slowly over the drain and notice what happens to the rods. Do they come together or move apart? People's responses can be different and either movement is acceptable. When you feel comfortable with the experience of the movement of the rods, go to the edge of the ground where you wish to locate the drain. Move slowly towards where you think it might be and wait for your rods to cross or move apart. When they do, mark the position on the ground using a peg. Next, stand in that position and, attuning to the alignment of the drain; inwardly ask your rods to point in its general direction. The rods should then move to the right or the left. Again, mark this on the ground with a peg. Now go to the edge of the ground again but this time a little further up.

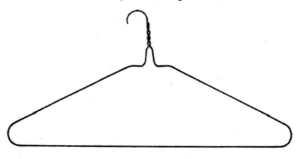

To make a pair of dowsing rods

You will need a pair of wire coat hangers

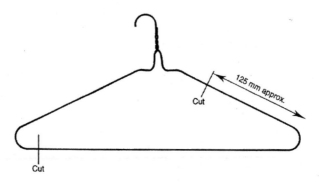

Cut each hanger in the position indicated with a pair of pliers

Bend each coat hanger to the above shape

Trying not to think of where you last experienced the rods crossing, wait for the rods to cross again and repeat the process.

After several repetitions, you will end up with a series of markers on the ground which ideally should all be in a straight line. But if not, try once more to assess the alignment of the drain run using the rods. The acid test now comes when you have to dig to locate the drain. If you do not hit it on one position of the line, try a little further along. If you are still not successful, you may have to keep digging the trench until you locate the run. Notice how far off-target you were and whether your alignment matched that of the drain run. Inexperienced dowsers will sometimes pick up a halo effect from the underground object that they are searching for, which causes a response several feet from the correct position.

A good dowser should be able to locate a drain run of this sort nine times out of ten. Occasionally, other objects such as cables, springs or energy lines get in the way, causing inaccurate responses. As with all techniques of this type, regular practice is important.

THE FORKED STICK

This is the traditional tool of the dowser but it is not used so extensively today, as it is quite a difficult technique to master. Originally a 'Y'-shaped hazel twig would be used because its wood is very pliable, but most dowsers using this method today choose plastic as a substitute.

Two approaches can be adopted. The first uses a plastic equivalent of the rod which is gripped with the whole hand. The second uses much finer plastic strips which are held between the thumb and the first two fingers. The use of either of these methods is more easily demonstrated than described in writing as it is dependent upon getting exactly the right feel and muscle tension which allows the stick to move. Whichever system you wish to use, you will first have to make your plastic strips.

The easiest strips to make are based on the plastic strips used to secure packing cases or boxes. Ideally, these strips should be 12.5 mm wide although the ones that I have are only 8 mm. You will need to cut two lengths, approximately 200 mm long, and then tape one end of each strip together using insulating tape or something similar. The skill of this method involves achieving the right tension in the plastic which will involve some experimentation on where to hold the two ends of the strip.

Firstly, stand upright and tuck your elbows tight into your sides, turning your palms upwards. Now tuck your ring and little fingers down onto your palm, and then bring your thumb and index and middle fingers together, pointing upwards. In this position and without the strip of plastic, move your wrists closer together and then further apart, pivoting at the elbows (tucked into your sides). This may seem a little awkward but gives the feeling of how you set up the tension in the Y-shaped plastic strip. Next, hold the strip in your fingers with the taped end pointing away from you. You will need to hold each end of the strip about half-way along and pinched between the thumb and the index and middle fingers. Now move your wrists closer together and eventually you will reach a point where a tension is built up in the plastic strip which inclines it to move up or down. Keep practicing with this tension and you will get the feel of the point where it could easily move either one way or another. This requires sensitivity with the grip. This point of tension is dependent upon the quality and thickness of the plastic being used. If you do not seem to be having much success, slightly rotate your thumbs in an outward direction which will cause a greater tension in the plastic.

The idea with this method is to hold the strips in such a way that this tension is constant, but where any slight movement will tip the strip up or down. You will notice that the slightest movement in your thumb will have this effect. This movement will indicate when you have crossed an underground object. The procedure of walking slowly over the ground is exactly the same as for the rods. Providing the right tension is held, your plastic strips will flip up or dip down in response to what lies beneath your feet.

'Y' RODS

The principle behind the Y rods is exactly the same as for the strips, the only difference being in the thickness of the material and the level of tension. My Y rod is made of two round pieces of flexible plastic 450 mm long, with the ends held together by two copper rings. The first ring is about 40 mm from the end and the second about 150 mm. Instead of being held between the thumb, index and middle fingers, these rods are held by the whole hand with the palms turned upwards. You will need to keep your elbows into your sides as before and to set the tension in the rods by slightly twisting your wrists together. These rods create a much greater tension and holding them can be more tiring. As before, slight movements in your wrists and hands will cause the rods to tip up or down.

Some people's bodies respond very easily to psi stimuli. Such people will find all aspects of dowsing very easy. If, however, you are not one of these people, one of the other levels of the psi spectrum will probably operate for you. You may, for example, more easily pick up clairvoyant pictures or hear clairaudient messages. Dowsing can be fun and also extremely accurate if you can master its techniques.

KINESIOLOGY

Kinesiology is another form of psi receptivity, based upon accessing the body to gain insights into the health and well-being of the person. It was developed by Dr George Goodheart from the USA and uses muscle strengths to determine the underlying causes of imbalance. It has been discovered that muscles will register as strong or weak depending upon what questions are put to the person, or what physical substances are introduced into their environment.

Anyone who has been muscle-tested in this way will know how extraordinarily different the muscle strengths can be when exposed to specific questions or outside stimuli. When testing for allergies, any adverse substance introduced onto the tongue, or placed near the patient, will immediately cause an arm muscle to go 'weak'. No amount of willing one's arm to be strong will work. Remove the offending substance and the arm returns to its normal strength. This method demonstrates how easily we are affected by the foods that we eat and by harmful substances in our external environment.

This form of testing is best carried out with another person and the usual method is to hold the arm out from one's side and for your partner or therapist to apply gentle pressure to the arm to test its strength. The substance that you want to test is then placed near you or a question is asked and the muscle is tested again. If the muscle goes weak, then an adverse reaction is indicated. Keeping one's arm out to the side of your body can be tiring and another method has the patient lying on a therapist's couch with one arm raised vertically. The therapist then pushes against this arm to test for a response.

The system can be used for answering all types of questions, not just analyzing imbalances within the body, emotions or mind. It is important, however, to check the polarity balance of the body as sometimes something called switching occurs. In this case, the polarity reverses and what tested weak now tests strong and so on. Moreover, in another therapeutic use of these methods, by deepening the questions being asked, a reversal of polarity also occurs. This can become quite complex and I would strongly urge anyone who wishes to explore these systems further to take a proper course. It is worth noting that polarity switches are quite common, which is why you should always test yourself each time you start this form of testing.

INTERNAL AND EXTERNAL SYSTEMS OF PSI RECEPTIVITY

In the last three chapters, we have explored the many different internal systems of psi receptivity. It is true that dowsers use physical implements to magnify their receptivity, but I see this still as an internal system. In the rest of this section, we will look at some of the many different external systems, such as numerology, the runes, tarot and so on. These systems should be used in conjunction with the internal methods, but they help by making some of the patterns that surround a situation or question external.

CHAPTER 11

Numerology

This system of divination has generally received the most scant regard by scientific researchers, yet it is of ancient origin. In this chapter, we will explore how by deciphering your date of birth and your name you can get insights into some of the dynamics of your life and personality. To understand how and why it appears to work we need to appreciate how numbers were perceived by ancient peoples.

THE MYSTERY OF NUMBERS

It is fanciful to imagine that at some stage in the dim past a caveman or cavewoman first realized the significance of counting. Like language, numbers and mathematics have helped human beings start to make sense of the world in which we live. In recent times, Einstein's equation $E = mc^2$ set the world alight with its implications. It was quite natural therefore that, to past peoples, numbers should assume a form of magical significance, which still has an echo in many Christian festivals and beliefs. Cultures evolved different counting systems and certain numbers took on special meanings. For example, the number 7 is used today for the days in a week, stemming from the biblical description of the creation of the world. It is also used in the calculation of the circumference and area of a circle, using pi = $^{22}/_7$. Coincidentally, seven is also the number of the chakras in Vedic tradition and the number of colors Sir Isaac Newton used to divide the color spectrum. The most famous monument of the ancient world, the Great Pyramid of Egypt, is based on a triangle with a height to base ratio of 7:11. Its association with the days of the week almost certainly arose from the division of the lunar month of approximately 28 days into four equal segments relating to the four phases of the Moon.

ANCIENT SYSTEMS

One of the most influential of all past philosophers was the Greek sage Pythagoras, who worked out the mathematical ratios in musical harmony. Number and sound became woven together in explaining the deeper meanings of the universe. Pythagoras is also reputed to have established a system of numbers related to the Greek alphabet, so that specific words and names could be reduced to their number equivalents. It is not known whether Pythagoras invented this system or borrowed it from another tradition. Certainly, there is a similar idea in Jewish culture, lost in the mists of time, called Gematria. Every letter of the Jewish alphabet was ascribed a number and these were incorporated into a system of knowledge based on the sacred quality of certain numbers. The hidden meaning of a word could then be translated by those who knew the key. It is these concepts that have been incorporated into the modern ideas of numerology.

Numbers were believed to reflect natural rhythms, and certain ratios like the Fibonacci series 0, 1, 1, 2, 3, 5, 8, 13, 21, 34, 55 etc. (where the sum of the preceding two terms gives the next, e.g. 3 + 5 = 8) can be found in the natural world. For example, the spirals on a sunflower both clockwise and anticlockwise, are always two consecutive numbers from this series. The ratio of any two adjoining numbers in the sequence is a very close approximation to the 'golden mean' proportion of Greek architecture found in the Parthenon in Athens and many other similar monuments. Numbers quite naturally took on a sacred character, and tradition has passed down to us the esoteric meaning of single-digit numbers.

NUMEROLOGY TODAY

Numerology in the West today is derived from these ancient ideas. It uses both the date of birth of an individual as well as their common name to make its interpretation. Before looking at these ideas in more detail, two concepts need to be understood. First, every number, no matter how large, can be reduced to a basic single digit number. For example, the year 1995 can be reduced as follows: 1 + 9 + 9 + 5 = 24; 2 + 4 = 6. Six would then become the key number for this particular year. Further interpretations could be made by examining how this number was derived. The repetition of 9 and the intermediate steps of 24 could be analyzed for further meanings.

Secondly, although single digits are the basis of numerology, certain composite numbers were also regarded as special. Principally, these involved any repetition of digits such as the numbers 11, 22, 33, 44, 55 and so on. The infamous number 666 found in the Book of Revelations contains a hidden code. Incidentally, the number 666 appears in the Bible three times. In Kings 10:14 we read, 'Now the weight of gold that came to Solomon in one year was six hundred, three score and six talents of gold.' This whole verse contains hidden messages. Solomon stands for the sun (sol) and the moon (omon), and the year represents the cycle of the sun through the zodiac. The element gold is also traditionally associated with the sun. The factors of the number 666 contain many interesting insights and, when reduced numerologically to 9 (6 + 6 + 6 = 18; 1 + 8 = 9), contain other meanings. If you read the Bible in this light you will find many additional meanings.

LETTERS TO NUMBERS

It is very doubtful whether the English alphabet we know today was ever deliberately linked to a number system in the same way as the

Hebrew alphabet. However, a common system has emerged which is based on a simple system of associating one of the numbers between 1 and 9 with the position in which the letter falls in the alphabet. For example, M is the thirteenth letter of the alphabet and has therefore been ascribed the number 4 (1 + 3). The complete list is as follows:

1	2	3	4	5	6	7	8	9
A	B	C	D	E	F	G	H	I
J	K	L	M	N	O	P	Q	R
S	T	U	V	W	X	Y	Z	

To ascertain the numeric equivalent of any name or word, simply substitute the letter for a number and then reduce the numbers to a single digit. For example, my name David is composed of the numbers 4, 1, 4, 9, 4, which reduces to the number 4 (4 + 1 + 4 + 9 + 4 = 22; 2 + 2 = 4). In this name, the number 4 is repeated three times and its sum total is also 4. Moreover, adding the numbers together gives 22 which is a repeating digit number. All these factors would be used as an interpretation of the qualities that lie behind this name. Write down your own first name and see what it reduces to.

To make a full interpretation, you will need to write down the full name by which you are commonly known. If you are normally known as Dick Humpheries not Richard Humpheries, then base your assessment on the former name. You will eventually arrive at a single digit for each name. These can then be independently assessed and then added together. For example, my second name Furlong adds up as follows: 6 + 3 + 9 + 3 + 6 + 5 + 7 = 39; 3 + 9 = 12; 1+2 = 3. So, as David = 4 and Furlong = 3 the key number for my name is 4 + 3 = 7. Before proceeding further, work out the key number for your full name.

DATE OF BIRTH

Leaving aside all arguments about the changes in the Gregorian calendar and the arbitrary way that we have arrived at the present year on the basis of the assumed date of Christ's birth, it is normal practice to use the full birth date in assessing your destiny number. So, for example, if you were born on 21 July 1948, your birth date would be written down as 21: 7: 1948.

There are different ways that we can add these numbers together. We could add 2 + 1 + 7 + 1... and so on, or we could add 21 to 7 to 1948. Whichever system you choose, you will eventually end up with the same single number, in this case 5. The system that I normally adopt is to obtain a key number for the year which in this case is 22 or 4, and then add this to the other numbers of the date, in this case 21 + 7 + 22 = 50.

I would assess whether there was anything significant about this number before reducing it to its single-digit form.

TRADITIONAL NUMBER MEANINGS

All numbers have both a beneficial and a detrimental aspect, depending upon how their symbolism is incorporated into the psyche. Indeed, in the course of our life, we may well end up acting out some of the extremes of these patterns. Use the numbers as a guide to give insight into your life and those of your friends or family. I also know of some counselors who check their clients' numbers to gain an insight into some of the underlying patterns that may be weaving through an individual's life. Such insights can be enormously helpful. I once heard a well-known psychologist say that she had spent 12 months regularly seeing someone with some deep psychological problems and building up a profile of the underlying causes of her condition. One day, the client presented an astrological profile which had been achieved in one appointment. It not only confirmed all the conclusions that the psychologist had taken a year to arrive at, but added much more detail that subsequently proved to be correct. Although rationally such concepts are impossible to explain in terms of known physical laws, empirically they will give some fascinating and helpful insights. One might argue that astrology is a more understandable system of character revelation than numerology, yet its basis is no more scientific. Both systems are dependent upon patterns that at some level give additional meaning to and greater comprehension of a situation or person.

INTERPRETATIONS

NUMBER ONE

This is the first of the sequence and therefore carries the primary dynamic of positive creativity. It is the top and is associated with the life-giving energies of the sun. Number One people have enormous drive and energy, if they have harnessed this quality fully into their lives, which can carry them to the top. The number 1 also looks like an 'I' and the ego element of this number can sometimes cause problems, inducing the person take unnecessary risks. Such individuals can also be very self-centered. Yet the expansive quality of this number can radiate magnanimity to all those who are touched by its power. This generosity of spirit can enthuse others, getting the best from colleagues and friends.

- **Key words:**
independent, dynamic, original, ambitious, ego-centered, dictatorial, lazy, selfish.

Number Two

This is the first of the even, or Yin, numbers and reflects the passive qualities of sensitivity, introspection, calmness and adaptability. The Pythagorean school is said to have regarded two as a difficult number and I have found that people in whom this number is dominant often have problems running through their lives which can carry a fatalistic feeling. Well-balanced Two people have great insight and an ability to see both sides of a situation. This can sometimes mean that they have difficulty in acting decisively. Twos are ruled over by the moon, which waxes and wanes in terms of the light that it gives us. It affects our emotions and moods, sometimes taking us to the heights or dropping us into the depths of emotional turbulence. This lunar association figures strongly with those who have two emphasized in their numbers. Twos can be very protective of those who are close to them, rushing to their defense regardless of the consequences. This protective quality can sometimes become over-possessive and stifling, leading to jealousy if the object of their desire turns his or her attention elsewhere. This number has powerful transformative qualities if harnessed correctly.

- **Key words:**

reflective, passive, calm, insightful, transformative, sensitive, psychically receptive, protective, jealous, moody, pessimistic, introverted.

Number Three

Three forms the last leg of a triangle that stabilizes the first two numbers. Trinities are very important which is why they are represented so extensively in mythologies and fairy stories. Three people, like Ones, have great drive and perseverance but this generally has a less self-centered quality than their One counterparts. They are explorers and their innate vitality acts as a platform that allows them to delve into many different aspects of life. They have enormous enthusiasm for all that they do, and an optimism which empowers them to take on great challenges. They can be serious when necessary, but also enjoy humor and practical jokes. Three people do not like being tied down to mundane routine, except where this serves some larger cause. They like activities that continually stretch their skills, whether it be mental, emotional or physical. On the more difficult side, they can sometimes be too independent or aloof, and lacking in responsibility, self-reliance or any sense of moral obligation.

- **Key words:**

optimistic, happy, fun-loving, inquisitive, exploratory, persistent, irresponsible, extravagant.

NUMBER FOUR

Four allows for great vision but also has a practicality that can bring this into physical reality. Individuals in whom this number is emphasized can be very artistic, with a natural sense of beauty and form. Their inner perception of order and harmony encourages the determination to see this expressed in their outer world. When the higher vision is clouded, this quality sees only practical forms which can make them dogmatic and stubborn. They make good business partners and often have excellent mental powers, with a single-mindedness that can carry projects through to completion. The difficulty with this perception is its sometimes blinkered nature that results in a failure to take all factors into account. It is reminiscent of the adage, 'The end justifies the means'. They have a good ability to generate or acquire money from all sorts of sources and have a resourcefulness that makes them excellent survivors. They are not deterred by routine and they can be passionate lovers.

- **Key words:**
  practical, single-minded, artistic, clear-thinking, narrow-minded, dogmatic.

NUMBER FIVE

Five is the number of communication, travel, education and balance. Those with five dominant will often be restless, always seeking new pastures. They have an ability to take experiences to extremes in order to understand the innate nature of balance and harmony. They often have excellent minds, which will be continually directed to acquiring more knowledge and information. They can be powerful communicators, with a gift of persuading others to their cause, which also makes them good salesmen. Sexual experiences are seen as adventures, which often means that they are not faithful lovers, unless variety is continually found within the partnership. They dislike routine intensely and prefer mental pursuits to physical tasks. They generally enjoy life, living it to the full in a versatile, progressive way. They also have a natural sense of justice and will rigorously defend any cause that they espouse, but their ability to see both sides of a picture will sometimes mean that they will take a reverse view the following week. This gives the appearance of inconsistency, which others find bemusing, but actually expresses the fascination that Fives have for exploring both sides of a polarity.

- **Key words:**
  communicative, versatile, clever, intelligent, quick-witted, self-indulgent, inconsistent, irresponsible.

NUMBER SIX

To the Pythagoreans, six was the perfect number, representing divine order and harmony. It expresses the 'love principle' in all its manifestations. Those with six in their numerological patterns will dislike arguments and dissent at all levels. Their primary task is to create harmony in all that they do, often serving others at their own expense. They are generally gentle, caring people, happy with routine and the simple tasks of life. Sexual relationships have to involve the emotions to be satisfying; if this is so, they will be faithful, expressive partners. Yet the search for perfection will sometimes make life difficult for them, leading to doubt and a lack of self-worth. Six people can also be self-indulgent, liking all the good things in life: a comfortable home, beautiful partner, gourmet food and the best wines. On a practical level they can be good organizers and administrators.

- **Key words:**

  beautiful, harmonious, loving, unselfish, tolerant, jealous, pessimistic, cautious.

NUMBER SEVEN

Seven is the number of mysticism, psychicism and spiritual wisdom. It also incorporates all the hidden aspects of life. Those in whom this number is dominant will spend much of their time in reflective thought, caught up in the richness of their imagination. They will also often be very psychically aware people, having an ability to pick up others' thoughts or intentions easily. This sensitivity can make life difficult for them, encouraging a retreat from the outer world to the inner. We all need to day-dream from time to time, but those with seven emphasized will often prefer to live in their fantasy world. This link with the unseen can also express a great spiritual perception, and recognition of the importance of meditation as a spiritual practice. Because of the strong link with the inner world, Seven people can appear to be distant and standoffish, making few friends. Yet those that are close to them will find a loyalty and affection that is very deep. The difficult aspects of this number express themselves through lethargy, depression and disillusionment, which sometimes cause a deep bitterness. If not also harnessed correctly, these energies can lead to alcohol and drug abuse. It is a number that allows you to reach the heights of spiritual awareness at one moment, only to plunge you in the depths of despondency the next. If a balance can be found between these extremes, I believe that the peace and serenity expressed on the face of Buddha will be yours.

- **Key words:**

sensitive, perceptive, psychic, peaceful, affectionate, introverted, addictive, secretive, ungrounded.

NUMBER EIGHT

Eight represents the completion of a cycle and, as its symbol turned on its side (∞) indicates, it connects us to the infinity of the cosmos. It links heaven with earth and allows for the grounding of spiritual principles in the physical world. Intuition and creativity of ideas are strongly emphasized, as is an ability to foresee the pattern of events in the future. Eight people often struggle with the dynamic of grounding their visions and may constantly seem to be battling against adversity. Yet the strength of this number will usually mean that they triumph in the end. When not engaged in one of life's battles, they can express a joy and happiness that is very infectious and will generally enjoy dancing and music. They have great courage and an ability to rise to the top in whatever career or profession they choose.

- **Key words:**

determined, intuitive, independent, innovative, joyful, creative, stubborn, dictatorial, intolerant.

NUMBER NINE

Those in whom this number is emphasized can present many paradoxes in their characters. This is the last single-digit number in the decimal system of counting and is a bridge between primary archetypal forms and their expression in the outer world. How an individual manifests this energy will be dependent upon his or her relationship with the other numbers in their character. Properly integrated, this number indicates someone who has achieved or has the potential to achieve a great deal in their life. It indicates the ability to be able to see beyond the materialistic to higher motives and aspirations. However, if these energies are not balanced, there can be a tendency for the more destructive aspects of the self - fear, greed and intolerance - to come to the fore. This number gives tremendous vitality to any event or aspect of life, and because of this it should always be examined in conjunction with the other numbers.

- **Key words:**

vital, self-expressive, positive, wise, courageous, impatient, indiscreet, impulsive.

OTHER NUMBERS

The only other numbers worth bothering with in a basic interpretation are those with double digits, such as 11, 22 or 33. To interpret these numbers, assess both their individual digits and the sum of their composition. For example, 11 expresses a double 1, so there would be tremendous drive and positivity directed into a dualistic perception of life (2). Any activity would almost certainly be carried out with an intensity and passion that would be very powerful.

MORE DETAILED INTERPRETATIONS

Once you have analyzed your birth date and name, there are two more levels of interpretation that you can obtain. These involve separately adding up the vowels and the consonants of your full name. The vowels will give your heart (emotional) number and the consonants indicate your general personality. There are therefore four levels to numerological interpretation that can be summarized as follows:

- **Destiny number:** derived from your date of birth, this indicates the karmic patterning of your life. It conveys the deeper meaning, destiny and purpose that you need to discover to express your spiritual self; the song that you need to sing to be fulfilled.

- **Key number or life plan:** obtained from all the letters of your full name, this indicates the dominant way that you approach the objectives of your life plan. It relates to the primary impulse that is you.

- **Heart number:** obtained from the vowels of your full name, this portrays your emotional expressions and the more passive aspects of your being. It is sometimes connected with the expression of your soul as opposed to your ego.

- **Personality number:** obtained from the consonants of your name, this relates to how you tackle events in your life. This expresses the ego or outer side of your personality rather than deeper impulses from within.

INTERPRETATION EXAMPLE

Let us use Winston Churchill, who was born on 30 November 1874, as an example. Firstly, his life plan destiny number from his date of birth is 7 (30 + 11 + 20 = 61; 6 + 1 = 7). This is a number associated with the mystical side of our nature. It links with intuitive perceptions, alcohol, spiritual awareness, and mood swings. Churchill's name breaks down as follows:

W	I	N	S	T	O	N		
5	9	5	1	2	6	5	= 33	= 6
C	H	U	R	C	H	I	L	L
3	8	3	9	3	8	1	3	3 = 41 = 5

Life plan	=	6	+ 5 = 11	
Heart	=	19	= 10	= 1
Personality:	=	55	= 10	= 1

Eleven is one of the special numbers and indicates a powerful potential. His first name also contains a double 3, which also adds power to his personality. His heart number is 1 and his personality number is initially 55, which then reduces to 1. Again, we have the double digit 55 for his personality. Five is the number of communication, so we would expect to find that this person is a powerful communicator. The emphasis on 1 gives an enormous drive and will to succeed and an ability to reach the top. Churchill believed himself to be a man of destiny, an impression which these numbers certainly reinforce. The depression that dogged him throughout his life is emphasized by his destiny number, 7.

CONCLUSIONS

Using numerology will give you some deeper insights into your own character as well as those of your friends. If you are starting a new project, you may wish to check whether its date gives the right numerological flavor to your intentions. Astrologers will also suggest that you do not start certain projects until the influences are beneficial. On certain occasions, when starting a new project, I have made sure that both the astrological and the numerological patterns were appropriate.

CHAPTER 12

Reading the Runes

The spiritual impulses that permeate this planet find expression in all cultures. In the UK, the two main streams of influence, apart from Christianity, stem from the Celtic and Norse traditions. The Celtic dominates in the west, but where the land was invaded by the Vikings, Danes and Anglo-Saxons, there is an influence that stems from the Teutonic and Scandinavian mythologies. Some of the days of the week, for example, are named after Scandinavian gods or goddesses (Wednesday = Woden or Odin's day). The system of divination and magic that comes down to us from this culture is embodied in the runes.

The word rune comes from the German word raunen, which has been translated to mean cut or carved, indicating that the runes were carved on stone or cut into wood. An alternative suggestion is that the word means secret or hidden, indicating a magical power that lay behind the runes. Basically, the runes are an alphabet and were used to describe events in the lives of the people of those early times, in exactly the same way that we use alphabets today. Like many other pictorial alphabets such as the ancient Egyptian hieroglyphs, each rune has a specific meaning that is separate from its phonetic sound. The rune ◇ has the sound (ng) as in thi(ng) and also stands for 'fertility'.

The origins of the runes are lost in the mists of time. The earliest similar signs appear on the Hallristingnor rock carvings in Sweden, which have been dated to around 1300 BC. These show sun wheels, swastikas and other patterns that have a symbolic meaning. The runes, it would seem, developed over a long period, and were particularly influenced by the Romans. Eventually, an amalgam of sigil or symbol and phonetic alphabet took place.

MYTHOLOGY AND THE RUNES

In the Scandinavian myths, we are told that the runes were given to mankind by the great god Odin who hung for nine days in torment on the great tree called the Yggdrasil before he gathered up the runes. This myth is reminiscent of the ancient Egyptian myth in which the god Thoth gave hieroglyphs to the Egyptian people. The runes, having been bestowed by a god, held magic power that could be used for divination and spell casting. Casting spells is a form of projected psi influence and was used for healing, fertility and protection, as well as invoking higher influences to give victory in battle.

RUNIC ALPHABET

In its original Germanic form, there were 24 letters in the runic alphabet. These were divided into three groups of eight runes, each group being known as an aettir. Each aettir was held sacred to a Norse god: Freyer, Hagal (Heimdall) and Tyr. Figure 12.1 shows the three aettir, their letter equivalents and their symbolic meaning. The Runic alphabet is usually referred to as the *futhark* after the first letters in Freyer's aettir. For divination purposes, an additional blank rune is added to the twenty-four inscribed runes, making twenty-five in total. The blank rune represents fate or karma and is associated with the Germanic word *wyrd* (from which the English word weird comes) which stands for the power of fate, or divine influence, in our lives. The division of the runes into three groups of eight links each set to the eight universities of the quantum realm. Each university has been allocated three runes and their associations are shown in Figure 12.1.

DIVINATION TECHNIQUES

In all systems using symbolic representations such as the runes or tarot cards, there is a basic procedure for divination which changes very little. Firstly, it should be understood that all these systems only give an indication of the prevailing influences that surround any question or situation. They will not tell you how you will cope with a problem, nor whether it will actually arise. If you have a reading by someone else, do not rely on, or accept, everything you are told. I have known many situations in which predictions of dire things that were going to happen proved to be completely unfounded. I always prefer my students to carry out any readings for themselves and to see this as a way of accessing their higher wisdom. If difficult cards or runes come up, look at this as a warning of something that needs to be addressed or faced up to. Whichever system or systems you choose, you will still need to use your discrimination and intuition in unraveling the messages. These systems will give you access to the quantum realm; how you use or interpret the information will be up to you.

With all systems, you will need to spend a few minutes centering and balancing your energies before connecting to your inner light then linking to the symbol of the Sun or your higher guidance. These little inner rituals are very important in ensuring that you give space to the deeper parts of your being to bring forward the right information for the situation. It is rather like making certain that you dial up the correct access codes on your computer. Punch in the wrong number and you could end up getting incorrect or misleading information. Having made your inner connections, you will then need to select one or more runes, cards or whatever; these are then set down in a sequence before you. Traditionally, a number of ways of laying down these symbolic items have evolved, which will be discussed later. But in practice it does not really matter how you lay out your runes or cards; their importance lies in their interpretation.

Runic alphabet

Freya's Eight

F	U	Th	A	R	K	G	W
Possessions	Strength	Gateway	Messages	Communications	Openings	Partnership	Joy

Heimdall's Eight

H	N	I	J	Y	P	Z	S
Disturbance	Restraint	Standstill	Harvest	Defence	Initiation	Protection	Wholeness

Tyr's Eight

T	B	E	M	L	ng	O	D
Warrior	Growth	Movement	The Self	Flow	Completion	Inheritence	Breakthrough
Red	Yellow	Orange	Green	Indigo	Magenta	Blue	Violet

At the most simple level, drawing just one rune when confronted by a problem or question will give some insight into its underlying patterns. This may counsel some positive action or give a caution, depending upon the question asked. It will still be up to you how you proceed from that point. If you are presented with a number of seemingly difficult problems when wishing to embark upon a project, challenge your divinatory system by asking it further questions. Maybe the timing is not quite right, or you may have omitted to think of some important factors that will influence the outcome. Asking the runes these sorts of questions will produce greater clarity in what you are doing. If all the indications still seem against the project, there is another way to elicit information, or ensure a good outcome, which will be fully discussed in the last section of this book.

FATE AND LADY LUCK

We are all fascinated by what our future may have to offer, even if at some level we are reluctant to know. The most important concept to appreciate is that your future is not fixed. Life is what we make it. It is true that certain patterns weave through our lives, and that once you have embarked upon a particular course of events it may be difficult to change the dynamic. If you get on a train headed for the wrong destination, it may be impossible to get off again once aboard until you arrive at the next station. In such situations, you may need to learn to accept where you are and, instead of fretting and complaining, to sit back and enjoy the journey. The only journey that lasts forever is the journey of your experiences; periods of ease and difficulty will come and go through your life. Part of the challenge of being human is learning to cope with the downs as well as enjoying the ups.

The runes and other systems of divination will indicate the trends of your life and, in that sense, outline possible future events. To every difficulty there is a solution and rather than ask to win the lottery, it is much better to ask for guidance in solving the problems that confront you.

MAKING YOUR RUNES

Traditionally, the runes should be carved on wood or stone. Sets of rune stones can be acquired at many shops, local bookshops or through the internet. If you do not wish to go to this expense, you can always draw the runes on a piece of paper or, perhaps more easily, on some small (14 x 9 cm) address cards. Some runes have a reversed meaning if they are upside-down, so you will need to ensure that the cards are oblong and not square. Once you have acquired or made your runes then you can begin.

DIVINATORY SYSTEMS

LEVEL OF QUESTION

In the Runic and Celtic systems of mythology, three levels of experience or consciousness were acknowledged. These relate to the spiritual, mental and physical realms. The first expresses the primary principles or patterns behind events and connects to our karmic and spiritual self and to relationships with others. The second is the realm of ideas, plans and projected events; the things that both inspire and impede us. The last realm relates to events in the physical world and includes success and achievements.

When you pose a question to the runes, it is important to know which of these three realms holds the answer. If you look at Figure 12.1, you will see that the runes are divided into three groups of eight which reflect the three realms although in a slightly different order. These are as follows:

- **Freyer's aettir**: love, happiness and spiritual growth.

- **Heimdall's aettir**: worldly achievements, money, power, success, sexuality and the physical realm.

- **Tyr's aettir**: mind, intellect, wisdom and self-transformation.

Although these realms indicate the broad principles that stand behind each group of runes, individual runes can still be interpreted on a spiritual, mental, or physical level. For example, the rune X (Gebo), which is part of Freyer's aettir and stands for partnerships, can relate to the relationship with our spiritual self, the connection to an idea, or a sexual liaison. To determine which of these levels is relevant, you will need to draw an initial rune which will then act as the overview and set the tenor for the whole reading. The aettir of this rune will indicate the level of the question being asked or, perhaps more accurately, the most relevant level for the answer.

THREE-RUNE METHOD

The next step after selecting your initial rune is known as the 'three-rune spread'. As we saw in Chapter 11, three has a special significance and also relates to the three layers of our being. Most pictorial languages are read from right to left, so in casting the runes the first would be laid on the right-hand side, the second in the middle and the third on the left. Each rune depicts an aspect of the situation or question being asked.

The first rune deals with the situation itself and, in particular, the events that have led up to it or lie behind it. The second rune indicates what action should be taken, and the third rune indicates the likely outcome. In some situations, the final outcome may show further problems, but these may be the necessary outcome of events already in motion. All that can be done in these cases is to follow the process through to its conclusion.

Further information can be gained from the three-rune spread by laying additional runes above or below one or more of the three runes.

Runes below the original line indicate factors on a physical level that are either supporting or impeding the situation. This might relate to people or to circumstances, such as money or physical surroundings. Runes laid above the line show spiritual, karmic or psi influences that are having an impact upon the situation.

RUNE DIVINATION EXERCISE (time: 10 to 15 mins)

Aim: To gain an answer to a question using the runes

- Sit in a relaxed position with the runes in a bag beside you.
- Attune within and connect to your inner light. Then feel that you are linking this light to the sun.
- Think of your question. You could write it down on a piece of paper.
- Put your hand into the bag and draw forth one rune which will then act as the significator or overview of the reading.
- Draw forth three runes and place them under the significator rune, moving from right to left.
- Look up the meanings of the runes and, by attuning within, try to interpret their message.
- If it does not seem clear, draw further runes as described below.
- Note down the runes and your conclusions beside the question.
- Before finishing, connect once more to the light within and close down.

These methods can be used or adapted for all sorts of questions and situations. There are more elaborate systems of rune divination but these methods will serve most purposes. One other system will be given in Chapter 15.

RUNE MEANINGS

The basic rune meanings are as follows:

- **Possessions** (Feoh): This rune covers everything that you have acquired in your life, on a physical, emotional, mental and spiritual level. It indicates that these aspects are being integrated into your being in the correct way, like the acquisition of the talents in the parable of Jesus. Reversed: Intimates that you are either misusing your gifts or that you are letting slip what once was yours.

- **Strength** (Ur): This rune represents the power to achieve what you are attempting but does not necessarily say whether you will be successful. Reversed: What is being sought is beyond your capability or the power is being misused.

- **Gateway** (Thorn): This is the rune of taking stock before you cross the threshold onto a new level. The gateway is the initiation door that has to be traversed before moving on to deeper insights and experiences in life. Initiation was always something that was approached with great care and with much preparation. When this rune appears, you are forewarned of a change in your life. Reversed: Do not make hasty decisions at this time.

- **Messages** (As): This is the rune of connection with the higher self and stands for the link into the quantum realm. Drawing this rune indicates that help from a higher level is available. Reversed: Some aspect of yourself is blocking or ignoring what is being offered.

- **Communication** (Rad): This is the linking rune, which connects you with individuals, nature and sources of help. There is always a two-way exchange indicated with this rune; you need to give as well as receive. It can also intimate physical journeys taken as part of an inner quest, such as a pilgrimage, or for the outer connection being made. Reversed: There is a breakdown in communication between yourself and another person or group of people. It may also indicate delays in your journeys.

- **Openings** (Ken): This rune lets you know that openings are appearing in your life, bringing new beginnings. It is a very beneficial rune and indicates the need to take firm action in seizing the current opportunities. Reversed: The dawn has not yet come and you will need to endure further. It may indicate that for a while things will get worse than they are at present. But in the cycle of transformation the dawn will surely arrive after the darkest hour.

- **Partnership** (Gebo): Marriages, unions and partnerships are covered by this rune. It represents the energy of uniting with what is outlined in the question. It may indicate uniting with the divine within or a friendship with another person. For partnerships to be successful there has to be a balance between the individual and the collective. Reversed: There is no reversal of this rune.

- **Joy** (Wynn): This rune indicates the joy that comes from fulfilling your objective. It takes the previous rune a stage further and expresses the energy that comes when we are united with the power of our true inner selves. Reversed: Represents the doubts and fears that stop us being ourselves. When this appears, you need to look at what is holding you back from being happy.

- **Disturbance** (Hagal): The rune starts the cycle of Heimdall's aettir. It indicates impediments or blockages that stand in your way and also disruptive events which will turn things on their head. In this sense, it is an awakener, shaking us rudely out of the slumber of our present lives. This is a powerful rune of change which sometimes gives the feeling that we are being swept along by external powers, over which we have no control. Yet ultimately all power lies within, and difficult circumstances leading to change will have to be faced. Reversed: It has no reversed position.

- **Restraint** (Nyd): This rune encourages us to look within for the solution to our problems, perhaps to confront some of the shadowy aspects of our personality. When this rune appears in your reading, constraint is indicated. Think well and deeply before you act for now is not the time for forward movement, such as starting a new project or applying for another job. Reversed: The forces of constraint lie outside you and you appear to have no control over them. This rune urges caution and patience.

- **Standstill** (Isa): This rune takes the pattern set by the previous two a stage further. Here, you are being urged to take stock in a positive way of all that is going on. This may involve surrendering part of your ego self to a higher cause or sacrificing some long-cherished desire. This standstill can cause deep frustration but patience is part of the lesson of this rune. It encourages self-reliance, which only comes from accessing your higher wisdom. Reversed: There is no reversed position.

- **Harvest** (Ger): After the inner transformative work of the previous two runes, here is the rune chart harvesting your efforts. It represents the cycle of the seasons through the year. Harvest is the time for celebration and renewal. It is the time to think about storing energy for the next cycle of growth. The saying 'make hay while the sun shines' expresses the sentiments of this rune. Reversed: There is no reversed position.

- **Defense** (Eoh): This rune encourages us to look beyond the outer manifestation of the situation to what is taking place at a deeper level. It suggests that there are outside disruptive forces in action which will attempt to impede you in what you wish to do. You need to be on your guard against these. It intimates that unexpected forces are moving around whatever question you are asking, and it is important to try to be aware of these for to be forewarned is to be forearmed. Reversed: There is no reversed position.

- **Initiation** (Peord): This rune is symbolic of the initiatory practices of the ancient Egyptians, where the neophyte was locked up in a tomb for three days and underwent a series of inner journeys. These demanded that they faced their deepest fears as part of their journey. The rune indicates the confronting of the self with all its shadowy aspects and the ability to move through fear. One of the greatest fears that many people have is of death. Confronting this fear is a symbol of this initiation. When this rune appears in your spread, take courage to face the fears that are holding you back. Reversed: Indicates an avoidance of what you need to confront. It also asks for a change of emphasis and way of doing things.

- **Protection** (Eolh): Invoking protection against outside destructive influences is part of the spiritual journey. This rune embodies the cloak of the divine mother shielding us from things that we cannot deal with on our own. In Greek myth, whoever the goddess Aphrodite bestowed her girdle on would be protected, even from the thunder bolts of Zeus. Aphrodite portrays love, the greatest protector. When this rune appears, know that protection is available to you as long as you ask for its help. Reversed: You are not spending enough time protecting yourself or your projects from disruptive outside influences.

- **Wholeness** (Sighel): This rune symbolizes the vitality of the sun, which nourishes and sustains life. It represents the circle of wholeness that bids us accept all polarities to achieve balance. This will bring forward the healing of any condition, even if this necessitates the death of the physical body, for in essence we are eternal. When it appears in a reading, this rune gives great power and expansion to what is being sought. Reversed: There is no reversed position.

- **Warrior** (Tyr): Some individuals battle continually against opposing forces. This is the rune of the warrior who struggles to overcome adversaries, whether they be physical, intellectual or simply difficult circumstances. Occasionally, the battles are with aspects of the self. This rune indicates the strength to overcome those forces that stand in your way. Implied here is also a sense of rightness and justice, and many who use the energy of this rune do so against wrongs of all types. Reversed: Inappropriate action or battles can lead to disaster. In this position, the rune preaches caution when taking on opposing forces.

- **Growth** (Boerc): This rune presages the right conditions for expansion and growth, depending on the question asked. It is a propitious rune, giving encouragement to proceed with your present course of action and confirming that everything is in place for events to come to fruition. The tree sacred to this rune is the birch, ritually used in the past to drive out the devil, which is why it was used to cane children in school. It therefore indicates that all negative influences have been removed. Reversed: Some aspect is blocking your growth or the expansion of a project. Check further to ascertain what it might be.

- **Movement** (Ehwis): This is the rune of transition and progress within situations, not from one situation to another. Within a relationship, it may indicate a new way of working with each other rather than a change of partner. Its energies are beneficial and uplifting, suggesting that all movement when this rune is drawn will be for the better. Reversed: Indicates blockages from within that need to be addressed.

- **The self** (Manu): This rune incorporates the rune of joy and its mirror image. It suggests that to find ourselves we need to acknowledge the polarity balances within. To discover joy, we must be prepared to experience sadness; for such balances produce eventual wholeness. This rune encourages you to accept the different polarities of your being. When it appears in a reading, always look for answers in the apparent opposites of the conditions before you. Consider all polarities very carefully before proceeding. Reversed: Blockages often come from within because we are not prepared to accept some aspect of our personality. When reversed, this rune indicates a failure to see all sides of a situation.

- **Flow** (Lagu): Connected with water, this rune represents the energy of fluidity that runs through any situation. It suggests the need to be open to moving with the currents of life through whatever event lies ahead. It advises non-resistance and acceptance. When it appears in a reading, accept whatever situation surrounds you and do not try to move away from it. In time, the river of life will take you into new waters without any effort. Reversed: Shows a resistance to what life is offering you.

- **Completion** (Ing): This rune presages the beneficial conclusion of any project, the point where all the hard work is appreciated fully, free from worries or doubts about its successful conclusion. This rune also relates to fertility and the potential for new growth and beginnings. This is almost always a beneficial rune, allowing us to savor our success. Reversed: There is no reversed position.

- **Inheritance** (Odel): This rune covers everything that we inherit from our parents, in the form of possessions and genetic traits. It links to our ancestral patterns and the different qualities of energy that come down to us from our forebears. On a material level, it can indicate your family home and heirlooms. It is also the rune of your extended family, your aunts, uncles and cousins. Reversed: Indicates separation from your family members or the loss of an inheritance. This may also indicate a need to break with the ties of the past.

- **Breakthrough** (Doerg): This rune brings to an end the Futhark. It represents the illumination that comes from the sun, dispelling the clouds of doubt that sometimes hem us in. It is the rune that gives us power to pierce the darkness with shafts of insight. It is the rune of intuition and the higher mind's ability to soar to new heights. When this rune comes up in your reading, it denotes that you will ultimately achieve your objectives. Reversed: There is no reversed position.

- **Fate** (Wyrd): Normal rune sets contain a blank rune that is said to stand for fate or destiny. This rune relates to the Three Fates of Teutonic mythology – Urd, Verdandi and Skuld, which represent time: past, present and future. When appearing in a reading it indicates some aspect of destiny that cannot be avoided. In this sense it relates to the Hindu concept of karma, yet this should not necessarily be seen in a negative sense for positive influences can come to us based upon past deeds.

RUNING YOUR NAME

The final piece of insight that can come from the runes is to see what influences are found within your name. You transpose each letter of your name with a rune. Some letters, such as 'c', do not appear in the Runic alphabet. Where this letter appears in your name, you will have to decide whether it is a hard or soft 'c'; soft 'c's (as in Celia or Cedric) can be transposed by the letter's'; for hard 'c's (as in Carl), you can use the rune letter 'k'. With V use the rune substitute 'th' (Gateway).

When you have written down all the runes, look up their meanings in the descriptions above to obtain an assessment of the influences connected to your name. This idea can be linked with the numerological interpretation in Chapter 11.

CHAPTER 13

I Ching

The I Ching is certainly the oldest of all the systems of divination that have come down to us. According to tradition, its origins and invention date back at least four thousand years, to the legendary Fu Hsi, one of the first divine emperors. Its ideas were later elaborated by Confucius, King Wen and the Duke Chou, and their commentaries and ideas are embodied in the present form of the *I Ching* or (as it is more accurately titled) *The Book of Changes*. As this could be said to be the Chinese equivalent of the Bible, it is a work of profound spiritual insight and wisdom, extolling individuals to discover the virtuous within themselves. In practical terms, it could be said to be the first systemized attempt to access the wisdom of the collective unconscious by accessing the eight universities of the quantum realm.

Fig. 13.1 – The dynamic flow of Yang and Yin

The I Ching is based upon the development of a very simple yet profound idea which is incorporated in the interweaving of two principles known as Yang and Yin. In essence, Yang represented everything that was outgoing, masculine and active, while Yin was receptive, feminine and passive. In Chinese belief, the whole of the cosmos was held in balance by the dynamic flow of energy between these two poles. The famous symbol that encapsulates this concept is called the Tao and is shown in Figure 13.1. When energy reached an extreme position, it would change onto its opposite and these flows held all creation together. It was therefore normal for the Chinese to classify everything as an aspect of one of these two principles, so, for example, under Yang would come the day, cold, dry, sky, man; under Yin we find night, hot, wet, earth, women and so on.

Two simple signs, a solid line (Yang) and a dashed line (Yin), were used to describe these two polarities. However, the Chinese were not satisfied with leaving the pattern at this basic level. The importance of a threefold development was recognized, so they expanded this basic idea by adding additional lines. The first stage was to add one other line, either Yin or Yang, to the first two, which would then create four possible alternatives:

Stage 1

Stage 2

The final step was to add a third line to the previous two, creating eight trigrams or principles that form the basis of the I Ching:

These trigrams were given specific attributes and were considered to be a family with father, mother and six children, three sons and three daughters. The symbolic meaning of each trigram is shown in the table. They also reflect the eight principles of the 'quantum' universities. Their meanings as recognized in Ancient China are as follows:

Name	Position	Image	Attributes
CH'IEN 	Father	Heaven	Creative, strong, active, firm, light, positive. *Spiritual quality*: universal consciousness & oneness.
CHEN 	Eldest son	Thunder	Arousing, excitement, growth, expansion. *Spiritual quality*: balance within evolution.
K'AN 	Middle son	Water	Danger, difficulties, Moon, enveloping. *Spiritual quality*: cleansing and transformation.
KEN 	Youngest son	Mountain	Stillness, waiting, immovable. *Spiritual quality*: inner perception.

K'UN ☷	Mother	Earth	Weak, yielding, nourishing, passive. *Spiritual quality*: divine love.
SUN ☴	Eldest daughter	Wind	Gentle, penetrating, gradual. *Spiritual quality*: meditation and reflection.
LI ☲	Middle daughter	Sun	Clarity, consciousness, illuminating, lightening. *Spiritual quality*: inspiring others.
TUI ☱	Youngest daughter	Lake	Joy, happiness, pleasure, openness. *Spiritual quality*: the joy of giving.

DEVELOPMENT OF THE TRIGRAMS

The eight trigrams were seen as representing eight primary principles that flowed through every aspect of life and creation. A system of association was established which became embodied in all levels of Chinese culture and was especially important in health and healing and the laying out of the landscape through a system known as Feng Shui. The eight trigrams were laid out in an octagonal sequence and each allocated a specific direction of the compass as shown in Figure 13.2.

THE ORACLE OF CHANGE

Having established the concept of the eight universal principles, the Chinese considered that further insight could be gained when any two principles were combined together. The combination of any two trigrams is called a hexagram and the 64 hexagrams form the basis of the I Ching's pronouncements.

For example, Hexagram 39 (Obstacles) is made up of trigram **K'an** (Danger) over trigram ☵ **Ken** (Keeping still). ☶

Another way of looking at this idea is that any situation or problem will be a combination of two principles, rather like the two sides of a coin. As we have said, the original insights propounded by Fu Hsi were elaborated by Confucius, King Wen and Duke Chou and it is these modifications that form the interpretations of the 64 hexagrams.

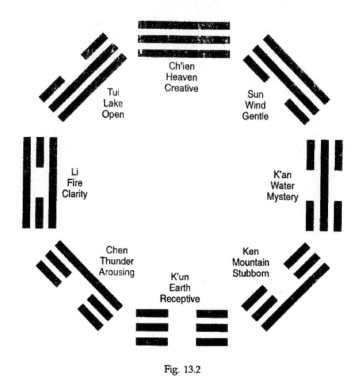

Fig. 13.2

Fig. 13.2 The arrangement of Trigrams in the Greater Heaven Sequence

If you analyze the above sequence you will see that it does not quite conform the same pattern we have established with the quantum universities. This does not matter for it is the principle of relating to these specific archetypes that is important. We will come across another version later in this chapter.

CASTING THE ORACLE

The original oracle was divined annually by the emperor to give insight into the prevailing conditions for the coming year. Its use was later extended throughout China, but it has always been held in high regard. This sense of reverence was an important part of the ritual of divination. A great deal of thought would be given to making sure that the question being asked was appropriately phrased and then the oracle would be cast by the divinatory. This was traditionally done using 50 yarrow storks, which would be selected in a specific way. This is quite a time-consuming system and today most people use the three-coin method.

THREE-COIN METHOD

To carry out this method you will need three identical coins. Some people keep three special coins for this purpose, which adds to the sense of ritual when they carry out the divination. It is normal practice to shake the three coins in the cupped palm of both hands before throwing them onto the floor or your divination table. You could shake the coins in a tumbler or similar container but it is important to hold the question in your mind while you do this. In this system heads normally represent the Yin principle and tails Yang. The coins are cast six times in all and the combination of heads and tails gives the six lines of the hexagram.

Three coins, thrown in this way, will give four possible combinations:

a) Three heads (Greater Yin)
b) One head and two tails (Lesser Yin)
c) One tail and two heads (Lesser Yang)
d) Three tails (Greater Yang)

It is clear why a) and d) represent Yin and Yang respectively. With b) and c) it is the single coin that determines the rulership so b) is Yin and c) is Yang. However, there is a further complication in that extreme positions were seen to be unstable and therefore likely to convert to their opposite. The three heads and three tails (Greater Yin and Greater Yang) were therefore considered liable to switch polarity, converting to their opposites. These are known as moving lines and formed an important extension to the divination process, as by changing these lines another hexagram could be created.

Yang/Yin associations with the four combinations are as follows:

a)	Three heads	**Moving Yin**	9	— — •
b)	One head and two tails	**Stable Yin**	8	— —
c)	One tail and two heads	**Stable Yang**	7	——
d)	Three tails	**Moving Yang**	6	—— •

These four sequences are often given the numbers 6, 7, 8, 9 as shown above in order to differentiate whether the line is stable or moving. Each throw of the coins would give one line of the hexagram, which is started from the bottom up. Let us suppose that you threw the sequence 9, 8, 6, 9, 7, 8. The 9's and 6's are moving and would allow the hexagram to be changed into a new hexagram for a further interpretation or outcome. In other words Yang lines become Yin and Yin lines Yang. A sample hexagram would be as follows:

8	— —		— —
7	——		====
9	— — •	would convert to	====
6	—— •	would convert to	— —
8	— —		— —
9	— — •	would convert to	——

This is Hexagram 39 **Obstacles**   This is Hexagram 17 **Adapting**

The first hexagram gives the present position in relation to the question being asked, and the second shows the final outcome. In a full divination, each of the moving lines also has an additional meaning, so that from just one series of coin casts, fairly full and specific answers can be given.

INTERPRETING THE HEXAGRAMS

The I Ching is couched in terms of how the 'superior' man/woman should act in any given circumstances. If you read early translations from the Chinese texts phrases such as, 'A superior man of modesty and merit carries things to conclusion' frequently appear. The oracle is appealing to the highest aspect of your consciousness and suggesting what is the most propitious stance for you to adopt in line with your inner wisdom. More recent translations tend to drop the emphasis on the 'superior' man but it is important to appreciate the level of aspiration behind the I Ching.

LOCATION TABLE

UPPER → / LOWER ▼	CH'IEN	CHEN	K'AN	KEN	K'UN	SUN	LI	TUI
CH'IEN	1	34	5	26	11	9	14	43
CHEN	25	51	3	27	24	42	21	17
K'AN	6	40	29	4	7	59	64	47
KEN	33	62	39	52	15	53	56	31
K'UN	12	16	8	23	2	20	35	45
SUN	44	32	48	18	46	57	50	28
LI	13	55	63	22	36	37	30	49
TUI	10	54	60	41	19	61	38	58

Fig. 13.3 Location table.

DISCOVERING YOUR HEXAGRAM

Having established the sequence of lines, whether Yang or Yin, that makes up the hexagram, you will then need to look this up on the Location Table shown in Figure 13.3. This will give a number for the hexagram: there are 64 possible combinations and a short interpretation of each is given below. Once you have looked up the relevant hexagram and read the text, you will need to reflect on the answer. In some cases, the answer can be fairly obvious but in others it requires more thought. Traditionally, it would not be normal to ask more than one question at a session, as the Chinese believed that answers demanded careful thought and attention to gain the correct insight.

However, I do feel that it is permissible to ask perhaps one or two additional questions if further information is required.

THE SIXTY-FOUR HEXAGRAMS

A brief description of each hexagram is given here. For more detailed information you will need to consult a full text. A number of recommended books are given in the bibliography.

1. **Creative power:** Success will come through your own creativity. Look within for the answers and you will overcome all obstacles.

2. **Receptivity:** Success will come through help from your friends and colleagues. Learn to accept situations as they present themselves. Let go of your resistances and allow blockages or impediments to become learning experiences.

3. **Difficult beginnings:** Success will only come through your perseverance through difficulties. The birth process is not easy but the struggle will bring its own reward. Once set in motion, we cannot easily stop some things happening although they may be painful. Patience is required here.

4. **Inexperience:** Success may be impeded by your inexperience. We all have to go through the learning process at different stages in our lives. The vitality of youth carries great power and will see you through to the end, even if mistakes are made on the way. Be tolerant of yourself and others when mistakes are made.

5. **Patience:** Now is not the time to act, as conditions are against you. Patience is required in the knowledge that sooner or later conditions will turn favorably for you. Look to the little things and the details of your life.

6. **Conflict:** The situation is pulling in two different directions and you cannot avoid conflict at some level. You may need to step back gracefully and accept that persevering in your present course of action will not be successful. Look within for the answer, knowing that considered retreat can bring eventual victory.

7. **Collective power:** Working with others offers the potential of great success, but this often requires careful organization and leadership. You will need to marshal your resources to achieve your objectives; this may entail others helping you with your projects.

8. **Unity:** To be successful, you will need to establish a harmony within. This will require further attention to accessing your higher wisdom by whatever methods are available to you. It is important to trust the processes of this time and, above all, to be true to yourself.

9. **Restraining influences:** Conditions are at present holding you back from speedy progress. The restrictions can be irksome but are a necessary part of grounding your plans. Stick to the task in hand, recognizing that success may only come in small ways at present.

10. **Treading water:** This is a time when correct firm action is required to prevent problems arising. Progress will eventually be made through persistent effort, although caution is urged. If you stopped treading water, you would drown. Being true to yourself and clear in your objectives, tackling the difficulties as they arise, will lead to success.

11. **Peace:** Harmonious conditions prevail, which will be reflected in all that you do. This is a propitious time, when you will be blessed by good fortune. Your projects and efforts will prosper if your intention is correct.

12. **Stagnation:** An impasse is blocking your growth. This usually arises because we have avoided facing a situation that confronts us. Avoidance brings stagnation and eventual collapse. Look within for the causes of the blockage.

13. **Friendship:** This is a time for connecting with others in friendship and openness. It may be that this will lead to romance or the start of a new project involving your friends. Happiness is indicated, providing that you are in touch with the dictates of your heart.

14. **Abundance:** Riches on all levels are potentially available to you at this time, providing you can reach out and grasp them. Abundance comes when we acknowledge our inner power to bring forward positive change. Providing this is carried out in line with the wishes of the higher self, great fortune will follow.

15. **Moderation:** Moderation brings success. Do not splash out on frivolous things. Cultivate humility and modesty in all that you do at this time, setting aside savings for times of need. Moderation means finding the balance within between the extremes of your character.

16. **Enthusiasm:** Enthusiasm is a divine, empowering gift. It can be easily transmitted to others. You need to connect with those who are enthusiastic about your aims and ideals, for this will lead to success and happiness.

17. **Adaptation:** There is a need to adapt to the prevailing circumstances rather than trying to change situations which are beyond your

control. Be true to yourself but also be open to what others have to say, particularly those with new ideas.

18. **Repair:** That which has been broken can still be mended. The situation may seem hopeless, but there is always the possibility of change. Do not give up hope, even if things seem hopeless. Sometimes we need to let go, in order to retain. It is also important not to become complacent at this time but to strive to repair that which has been damaged.

19. **Moving ahead:** Now is the time to stick to your principles and move ahead. Success is indicated if you can hold onto what you know to be right within. This hexagram symbolizes the beginning of spring, which holds the promise of new life and vitality,

20. **Contemplation:** It is important to take a long, hard look at all your endeavors and, in particular, everything that is relevant to your question. There is a suggestion that your inner perceptions are not quite on beam and need amending or expanding in some way. There are times also when we need to meditate before acting.

21. **Reform:** There is a blockage in the shape of someone or something that is impeding your progress. This needs to be sought out and changed. Such changes usually must come first from your own attitudes. Look to what you might be doing that is blocking your success and then change it.

22. **Grace:** This is the time to enjoy all that life has to offer, particularly those things which seem small and insignificant. This is not the time for great happenings, but for an appreciation of what creates harmony. Details are important and should not be neglected.

23. **Deterioration:** The situation that you are in will continue to get worse, leading to full disintegration. This is part of a natural cycle of birth, growth and decay. You need to proceed with great caution at this time, and to look to your own inner strengths for the wisdom to know how to proceed.

24. **Return:** The cycle has come full circle and is about to be repeated. Now is the opportunity to let go of old habits and ways of acting with others. It is time for a fresh approach in your relationships and activities, so setting the tenor for the next cycle of your life.

25. **Innocence:** Innocence speaks of a child-like simplicity and spontaneity, which lies at the heart of true creativity. This is a powerful time to connect to the wisdom of your inner child to guide you through your present undertaking. Examine your motives and do not be bound by convention or conditioning.

26. **Potential power:** A tremendous potential energy is available to you at this time, which will nourish all your endeavors. You need to establish a clear direction to harness it fully.

27. **Nourishment:** It is important to be open to receiving help from others, as well as to spend time nourishing what you have set in motion. Neglect leads to a withering on all levels. Be constructive in your comments about others, and seek support from those who will nurture you.

28. **Breaking point:** The situation is in extreme tension and likely to break at any moment. Radical change is necessary to avert this potential crisis; it is time for transformation and change. Transformation can only come through connecting to your highest wisdom.

29. **Danger:** The shadow of the self is reaching out to envelop you. The only way to move through this abyss is to face your fears on both inner and outer levels. You need to face and accept yourself, warts and all, as then transformation can occur. Danger may be present in your outer life from individuals who wish you ill. Be on your guard.

30. **Clinging:** Fire needs to be continually nourished if it is not to go out. Within us, this is achieved by clinging to our inner source to draw forth its wisdom and understanding. This is a moment for energy and initiative, knowing that connection to your inner fire will illuminate your objectives. Attending to this inner source of nourishment will bring good fortune.

31. **Attraction:** We attract to us that which is important for our development and growth. Paradoxically, both opposites and similars attract, and understanding this principle can help us realize why certain things are happening to us. Look to what you are attracting into your life at this time and change what you do not want.

32. **Continuity:** Seek that which is enduring rather than transitory and success will follow. The links from the past can be of positive benefit in the future if connected in the right way. This requires perseverance and steadfastness. Stick to your principles and do not let opinion cause you to change what you know to be right.

33. **Retreat:** At times, it is better to pull back rather than press on when prevailing conditions are against you; now is such a time. Success will come through strategic withdrawal rather than pressing forward. Look to the details and gracefully accept the necessity of pulling back. An apology may help resolve conflicts.

34. **Great power:** Here is a moment when great power is available to you. Power can be beneficial or destructive and it is important that

the influences that you wield are used wisely and constructively for the benefit of others. Over-use of this power will inflate your ego, leading eventually to a fall.

35. **Progress:** You are being revitalized at the moment by the rays of the morning sun that will energize your projects and aspirations, leading to great progress. New ideas will flourish, especially if they also benefit others. Support will come from all sides and may lead to promotion or advancement in your career.

36. **Darkness:** This is a time for accepting your present condition, without knowing what the final outcome will be. Your inner fire burns brightly but is hidden, as though you are travelling through a dark tunnel not knowing what is outside or lies ahead. This is a test of your character and strength: you need to press forward, trusting the process, but not knowing exactly where you are heading.

37. **The family:** This relates both to your physical family as well as your inner family, those different character traits that make you who and what you are. For harmony to be achieved, correct order needs to be maintained. Look to your family at this time for the answer to your problems.

38. **Opposition:** Forces are pulling in two different directions. Trying to resolve these conflicting dynamics makes life difficult. These patterns may be operating in your outer life, through disagreements with others. They will certainly be an aspect of your inner life, where parts of yourself appear to be pulling in opposition to each other. You need to accept these as being two sides of the same coin for resolution to occur.

39. **Obstacles:** The way ahead is beset with blockages that may be of your own making, but could also come from others who are opposed to your intentions. Danger is indicated here so you will need to proceed with extreme caution, protecting yourself at every level. You may need to look to wise counsel to help you through this period.

40. **Liberation:** Freedom to achieve what you have set your heart upon now lies within your grasp. But you must act decisively if you are to make the best use of the prevailing conditions. The chains of the past are being freed and all that has held you back is falling away. Look within for resolution, then step forward positively on your path.

41. **Decrease:** There will be an initial decline followed by success. It is important to remain true to your purpose and intent and to have confidence that everything will come right in the end. Adaptability is required and the recognition that all things have their season. You will need to go through a metaphorical winter before the spring arrives.

42. **Increase:** There is a beneficial flow of help and ideas available to you which will further your objectives or plans. Make good use of your time and persevere in the pursuit of your goals. There is particular benefit in all things that help others, encapsulated in the Chinese motto, 'To rule is to serve'.

43. **Breakthrough:** You are poised to make a great leap, but for this to be achieved you need to stick resolutely to your principles and aspirations. Be aware of your faults and try to correct them, by being open and honest with yourself. Do not over-burden yourself with new tasks, but accomplish first what is already in hand.

44. **Temptation:** There are influences around that are trying to deflect you from your present goals. Be guarded against placing trust in those who outwardly seem supportive, but are actually trying to undermine your position. You will need to espouse restraint at this time and not be lured by offers which, although enticing, are actually counter-productive.

45. **Gathering together:** This is the time to draw upon all your resources, both people and accumulated knowledge. Information needs to be shared and ideas pooled to proceed to the next stage. You may need to let go of cherished ideas that are out of step with the prevailing influences. Those around you will show you what is important and what is not.

46. **Advancement:** Success is indicated through inner realizations. It is important to assess the timing of your projects and to seek help from those who can give clear direction. This also may necessitate accessing your own hidden wisdom. The foundations have been well laid and there is every opportunity for great success at this time.

47. **Oppression:** You are hemmed in by many adversities and your reservoirs of energy are exhausted. It is very important that you look at your self-destructive qualities, which lie at the heart of your present difficulties. By sorting these through you will eventually achieve success, but this will not be an easy task.

48. **Sustaining energy:** We each hold the potential for limitless energy, which can sustain all our endeavors. To find this source you will need to dig deep into yourself, to face your shadow and access that point where the life energy is held.

49. **Revolution:** When situations become stuck or fixed, it sometimes requires revolutionary ideas to break the mould. These are never easy to assimilate and can cause distress and pain. We tend to fear change, but this is what is being demanded at this time, suggesting that nothing short of a complete revolution of attitude or belief will be sufficient to bring success.

50. **Nourishment:** Success comes from honoring your obligations and commitments. You have the resources to benefit others and in so doing you will benefit yourself. Be open to receive as well as give, in order to create a harmonious flow in your life.

51. **Arousing:** Conditions are imminent that will shake you in your present situation. This is a necessary step to move you forward on your evolutionary path. Sometimes violent action is necessary when we become stuck in a particular mode of thought. Be open to change, and know that despite your fears, beneficial opportunities will soon come into your life.

52. **Meditation:** In the hustle and bustle of life it is necessary to establish ways of accessing our higher wisdom. Restraining influences will encourage you to spend time reflecting and meditating on your present position. Be still and centered, knowing that the cosmos has both order and rhythm. You need to align yourself to the Tao (the inner way); to be a human being rather than human doing.

53. **Developing:** Progress at this time will be gradual, so do not look for big changes. There is a suggestion here of good fortune coming through marriage. This may be the marriage with one's higher self or simply a business partnership which will bring success. Take small steps, making sure that each aspect is consolidated before moving forward.

54. **Subordination:** Situations are around over which you have no control. Your only recourse is to submit willingly to the dictates of the prevailing conditions and allow yourself to be carried along by the flow of current circumstances. Do not resist but submit to what is being offered, knowing that ultimately it will be for your greater benefit.

55. **Abundance:** There is an indication here of an extreme position, with abundance being either beneficial or detrimental depending upon the circumstances. You stand at the ultimate point of the pendulum swing which is about to move in the opposite direction. Accept this time for what it is and recognize that all things are cyclical, reaching peaks and troughs, highs and lows.

56. **Travelling:** The traveler carries few belongings and is not bogged down by material possessions. Now is not the time to put down roots but to consider carefully what can be discarded to speed your journey through life. Do not make long-term commitments for these will impede your progress at this time.

57. **Gentleness:** Continued pressure, although gentle, can have great influence, allowing you to penetrate to the heart of any situation. Firm, gentle persistency is indicated, encouraging you to hold to what

you know to be right, even in the face of adversity. Patience, commitment and quiet determination will achieve great ends.

58. **Joyousness:** Happiness can be an elusive quality. It is found when we truly accept ourselves, for this leads to inner contentment. Such a state is continually shifting and demands that we allow space to move and grow within. Joy comes when we help others, for this feeds back on itself. Happiness is there for you at this time, but remember that it will only endure if founded on inner truth.

59. **Dispersion:** Difficult elements that have been blocking your progress can now be dissolved. To achieve this you will need to access gently your inner negative feelings and those destructive patterns from the past that have become embedded in your psyche. This will require perseverance but the rewards will be a renewed connection with your highest wisdom.

60. **Limitations:** Striving for perfection or seeking high ideals are worthy aspirations but they can be heavy task-masters if we do not recognize our limitations and imperfections. You are being asked to acknowledge your limitations, not take on what you cannot adequately accomplish, and accept those aspects of yourself that are not perfect. Failure to acknowledge this important principle will lead to suffering.

61. **Insight:** All great discoveries and achievements have their origins in an initial insight or intuition that cuts across conventional thought. There is much higher level help available to you at this time, which will further your aims and aspirations. Look for the hidden truth within all situations and you will start to become aware of the underlying currents that flow through outer events.

62. **Small things:** Higher goals are clouding the details. These are very important and should not be neglected. The greatest building in the world is dependent upon its firm, but hidden, foundations. You cannot start building from the top down, only the bottom up. Look to your roots, that which exists on a physical level and the small details of any situation.

63. **Completion:** The point of balance has been reached, but will inevitably move out of equilibrium with the passage of time. Do not be complacent, thinking that all is now achieved, for that is the point of greatest danger, when everything may come toppling down. Take steps to protect yourself from future difficulties by continually assessing your situation.

64. **Before completion:** The ideal state is never to arrive, recognizing the circular pattern of all things. Success comes in continually striving to improve what you are setting out to achieve, knowing that

the step will lead you back to the beginning once more. Yet all things change, so no two situations are ever identical. You stand both at the end and the beginning of a new adventure. Accept it with open arms.

FENG SUI AND THE BAGUA

Although not technically a method of divination a brief mention needs to be made about the Bagua and Feng Shui because of its relevance to the eight archetypes and the way that it is used to provide a sense of balance and harmony within the home.

Those that are interested in this subject will need to obtain a book devoted to the subject of which many exist today. In essence Feng Shui is simply a means of honoring the eight principles in a harmonious balanced way within a home, office or space and this is achieved by ascribing a set direction to each principle. For example, to the east is ascribed Ken, which covers health issues. This equates with the Green university, which also relates to your health. In a home that has been subject to a Feng Shui treatment pictures and ornaments are carefully chosen to represent the ideal balance for that principle. For example in the relationship corner one should ideally have a picture of yourself and your partner or perhaps a statue that represents a loving relationship. The following chart shows the Bagua and its associations. I have indicated the relevant quantum university.

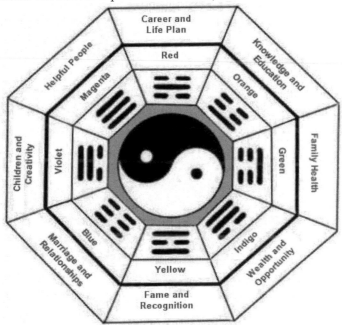

Fig. 13.4 The Bagua and its relevant associations.

Note: The above pattern shows north at the top of the page and south towards the bottom. In Ancient China they tended to put south to the top so you will often see the Bagua in a reversed position to that shown above. I have chosen this form as it most closely relates to the 8 universities discussed in chapter 5.

CHAPTER 14

The Tarot

ORIGINS

Compared with the two previous systems included here, the tarot is of fairly recent origin. Nevertheless is does beautifully portray the workings of the eight universities of the quantum realm and how we can utilize their influences in our journey through life. The earliest known cards representing divinatory pictures, similar to the tarot, date back to the late fourteenth century, but the tarot we know today did not emerge until the mid-seventeenth century. The tarot consists of 78 cards, divided into two groups known as the Major Arcana (22 cards) and the Minor Arcana (56 cards). The Major Arcana symbolize both archetypal influences as well as the initiatory steps that each soul must encounter at some stage in their life. The Minor Arcana is very similar to playing cards and is divided into four suits: swords, pentangles, cups and wands.

One of the most influential early authorities was Edward Waite, who was a member of the Hermetic Order of the Golden Dawn which was founded in 1888. Waite produced a pack and book in 1910 which set a standard for many tarot decks that have followed. I have drawn upon the symbolism of this pack here.

THE MAJOR ARCANA

The traditional names for the 22 cards of the Major Arcana are:

0.	The Fool	11.	Justice
1.	The Magician	12.	The Hanged Man
2.	The High Priestess	13.	Death
3.	The Empress	14.	Temperance
4.	The Emperor	15.	The Devil
5.	The Hierophant	16.	The Tower
6.	The Lovers	17.	The Star
7.	The Chariot	18.	The Moon
8.	Strength	19.	The Sun
9.	The Hermit	20.	Judgment
10.	The Wheel of Fortune	21.	The World

These twenty-two cards can be divided into three groups:
  a) Eight cards which represent the eight archetypes of the quantum realm

  b) Twelve cards which represent our initiatory journey through the twelve signs of the zodiac

  c) Two cards that represent our spiritual and physical self.

In the listing above the cards numbered 0 to 10 contain seven of the key archetypes of the quantum realm (see section on the eight archetypes below): these are the character cards of the Fool, the Magician, the High Priestess, the Empress, the Emperor, the Hierophant and the Hermit.

The remaining archetype, the Devil, is drawn from the second list. This accords with the tradition that suggests that the energies of one of these archetypes are not quite in balance with the rest, or perhaps reflects more of its shadow side than the others. This is why some mythologies have one character who is at odds with the others. In the Bible this was personified by Lucifer, whereas the ancient Egyptians called this god Set (from where we get the word Satan). Because of this concept, some esoteric schools encouraged their pupils to steer clear of this energy. However, we all have difficult or shadow aspects to our nature and these can only be resolved if we face them. By acknowledging and integrating the difficult aspects of our being, we find wholeness and balance.

As already stated twelve cards are associated with signs of the zodiac and represent an initiatory journey, rather like the twelve labors of Hercules. Their associations are:

Aries: The Chariot	Libra: Justice
Taurus: The World	Scorpio: Death
Gemini: Lovers	Sagittarius: Wheel of Fortune
Cancer: The Moon	Capricorn: Judgment
Leo: Strength	Aquarius: The Star
Virgo: The Hanged Man	Pisces: Temperance

The remaining two cards, the Sun and the Tower, are in some ways the keys to the whole pack. The Sun represents our eternal spiritual self, which has to incarnate into the material world, symbolized by the Tower, in order to grow. This latter card, often associated with the Tower of Babel in the Bible, shows how our inner self becomes easily divided while going through this process. The central quest of the self, through the initiatory journey symbolized by the other cards and assisted by the eight archetypal principles from the quantum realm, is to unite these separated parts. I would suggest that you obtain a Rider Waite set of cards to see the significance of the symbolism given below

THE INITIATORY JOURNEY

The journey starts with the **Chariot** whose twin horses, our Yin/Yang sides; need to be harnessed together for the journey to begin.

The winged disk, the symbol of initiation, is on the chariot, showing the central theme of the quest. The charioteer holds a rod of power in his right hand and has the star of illumination on his head. For initiation to be achieved, he has to venture into the **World**. This is both the last card of the Major Arcana and the first stage of the journey. It shows an idyllic view of life where the end is but the beginning and the beginning the end. The next card in the zodiac list, the **Lovers**, shows Adam and Eve, our masculine and feminine natures or animus and anima, stepping forth on their journey, acknowledging that trials and tests lie ahead of them. They are over-lighted by their guardian angel, whose wings stretch out to protect them. The **Moon**, the next card, is a symbol of sensitivity but also of illusion and delusion: the need to see through the distorted veil of outer reality to the truth that lies behind. To achieve our goals we need **Strength**, the next card, which comes from an inner recognition of the power that lies within all of us. The **Hanged Man**, the next card, represents self-sacrifice and the recognition that to achieve our objectives we have to take into account the needs of others. The trick in life is to find your bliss, as the mythologist Joseph Campbell advocated; to discover what really gives you joy and happiness and then direct that into helping others.

The next card, **Justice**, represents our karmic inheritance and the need for balance and letting go of past misdeeds. We can only do this when we truly accept ourselves for what we are, no more and no less. In order to find wholeness we need to let go of the attachments of the physical world. The card **Death** symbolizes this necessary but often painful process. It is the time for transformation and growth. When this is achieved, the **Wheel of Fortune** will turn in our direction, showing how cosmic forces will assist us. In the next card, **Judgment**, our guardian angel is shown blowing a horn in celebration of our re-birth or resurrection to our divine nature. The **Star**, with the eight points that illuminated the head of the charioteer in the first card, now shines down upon us. There are also eight stars on this card. The spiritual self, shown as a naked woman, is connected to all aspects of our being and the water of the self flows out from us to nourish the earth. The last card, **Temperance**, shows the transformed self, which has now become an angel, with the disk of illumination blazoned upon the forehead. The angel stands with one foot in the water and the other on the land, showing the need to link the spiritual and material sides of ourselves. A cup, the Holy Grail, is held in each hand, and water, representing spirituality, flows between them. A light shines forth from the mountains in the distance, indicating the journey that we have completed and the spiritual power that is now available to us.

THE EIGHT ARCHETYPES

The eight archetype cards throw additional illuminations on the eight universities of the quantum realm.

- **1. Initiation (Wisdom):** In the tarot, this is symbolized by the *Hierophant*. This is the card of spiritual power and illumination; the spiritual sun within the self. The Hierophant is the master of ceremonies, who conducts events for the benefit of the whole group. It is the card that leads us through the pathways of our initiations.

  Key words: Learning, initiation, professional advice.

- **2. Transformation (Courage):** The *Devil* card shows how we need to face all the shadow aspects of our personality. We can become easily chained to outmoded beliefs and patterns. This is an important part of our spiritual journey for we cannot overcome what we are afraid to meet within ourselves.

  Key words: Restriction, transformation, anger, fear.

- **3. Exploration (Faith):** The *Fool* embodies the child-like quality that allows us to explore life in an unfettered way. It preaches Christ's comment, 'Unless you become like little children, you cannot ever enter the kingdom of heaven'. The card shows a young man journeying forth accompanied by his dog (Anubis). It also combines one of the great initiations, that of trust. The Fool is about to step off the cliff but he does so trusting that he will be always be supported.

  Key words: Spontaneity, trust, adventure.

- **4. Formation (Clarity):** The *Emperor*, the symbol of worldly power and authority, watches over this university. He carries an ability to get things done in a practical, grounded way. It is important for that power to be exercised in a balanced way, symbolized by the rod and the orb, which he holds in his right and left hands. In ancient Egypt, the Pharaoh was always seen as an incarnation of the god Horus, who embodies this university.

  Key words: Responsibility, authority, promotion.

- **5. Communication (Integrity):** The ability to communicate with the quantum realm has generally been seen as a magical ability. The *Magician*, with his symbols of inner power and the sign of infinity over his head, carries this concept. This is the Merlin of the deck, assisting the King Arthur within us all to make connections with the wisdom that leads to appropriate action.

  Key words: Communication, intelligence, self-confidence.

- **6. Organization (Harmony):** The *Empress*, with her symbols of love and femininity, depicts this university. Twelve stars adorn her head and she holds a short scepter topped by a globe in her right hand, indicating her ability to hold sway over the spiritual and material worlds.

  Key words: Femininity, motherhood, sexuality, spirituality, security, domesticity.

- **7. Reflection (Peace):** The need to reflect inwardly, to meditate and find inner peace, is symbolized by the *Hermit*. There are times when it is important to retreat from the outer world of the senses into our inner realms and find connections with aspects of our being that we have forgotten.

  Key words: Withdrawal, seclusion, solitude, inner reflection.

- **8. Innovation (Vision):** Creative ideas and new insights were in the past seen as gifts from the gods. This university is symbolized by the *High Priestess*, who has the twin pillars of wisdom that support the temple of the self on either side of her. Her magical qualities are similar to those of the Magician.

  Key words: Intuition, wisdom, insight, dreams.

These eight cards can be used as gateways into the quantum realm if you so choose. The only one that needs to be approached with caution is the Devil, because of its associations with many of the shadowy aspects of human experience. Much the best symbol for this university is the white-winged horse Pegasus.

THE MINOR ARCANA

The 56 cards of the Minor Arcana express facets of our daily journey through life. These cards form the basic group for a divinatory reading. They are divided into four suits, like playing cards, which represent both the four elements and different aspects of human experience. The four suits and their associations are:

- Cups (water): Love, harmony, friendships, affairs, emotional matters and spiritual aspirations.
- Pentangles (earth): Material possessions, money, worldly achievements and the physical body.
- Swords (air): States of mind, conflicts, adversity, travel, learning and inner resolution.
- Wands (fire): Creativity, energy, dynamic action, intuition, insight, independence and initiative.

Each suit, like the playing cards, starts with the ace and is then numbered 2 to 10. The four remaining cards are the page, knight, queen and king. Each of these cards has its own symbolic meaning, which is interpreted differently depending upon whether the card is upright or reversed. Look up the meanings for the particular set of tarot cards you have chosen.

Tarot Card Decks

There are a large number of different tarot decks now available. They carry slightly different flavors but most follow the central themes given here. Selecting your deck has to be an individual choice, which should be made upon what you feel or sense within.

The Kabala and the Tarot

Before leaving this chapter something needs to be said about the link between the tarot cards and the Kabalistic Tree of Life and how the Tree relates to the Quantum universities.

The Kabalistic Tree is based upon ten spiritual principles which are called Sephiroth. These are set out in a special pattern (see Fig. 14.1), which indicates the way that these principles can be worked with in a meditative or inner reflective state: one principle leads on to the next and so on. The thesis presented in this book is that there are eight primary spiritual principles, which reflect out in every spiritual tradition so how can we equate the ten Sephiroth of the Kabala with this position?

Traditionally the tarot cards have been related to the twenty-pathways of the Kabala. However I have shown that eight of them: the Hierophant, the High Priestess, the Emperor, the Empress, the Fool, the Magician, the Hermit and the Devil relate or act as symbols for accessing the universities. These eight cards must therefore perforce also relate to eight of the Sephiroth and not just to the pathways on the Tree. Fig. 14.2 shows how this is done. The remaining two Sephiroth relate to two more tarot cards, the Sun and the Tower. As has been stated the Sun relates to our spiritual or divine self and equates with the central Sephiroth known as Tiphareth. The Tower on the other hand lies at the foot of the Tree in the Sephiroth known as Malkuth or the Kingdom.

The starting point for all meditative work on the Kabala is Malkuth and in order to access our spiritual self (Tiphareth) we need to progress by three possible routes, up the tree, via the Sephiroth known as Hod, Yesod or Netzach. The equivalent tarot cards here would be the Magician (Green university) the Devil (Red university) and the Hermit (Indigo university). The Middle Pillar is perceived as the hardest route for here the aspirant has to confront the shadow aspects of their being. The path through Netzach works with different meditation techniques, whilst Hod is the avenue of ritual magical practices.

This system has been in use for at least eight hundred years and perhaps much longer. It does reflect well our present condition which shows a separation between the soul part of our being and our 'ego' mind. Like many spiritual paths the novitiate has to undergo much inner work before accessing the true source of their being. The problem with such a system is that it becomes a self-fulfilling prophecy. If you believe that it is very hard to access the source of your inner wisdom then it will become very difficult. If on the other hand you believe that this is a birthright that anyone can achieve with just a little effort then everything becomes much easier. It is my perception that as we move forwards into the Aquarian epoch we will all be able to readily connect to those subtle spiritual aspects of our being: a New Age surely demands a new 'Tree'.

It is my belief that the old Kabalistic pattern has served its purpose and we can now work with a new matrix that does not separate the mind from the soul. I have called this the 'Aquarian Tree' and it is shown in Fig. 14.3 complete with some easily remembered access symbols.

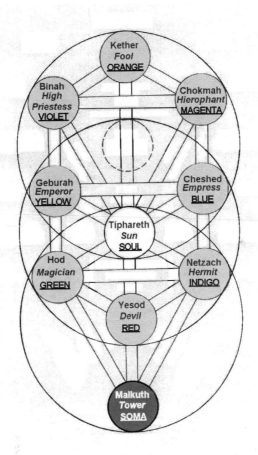

Fig. 14.2 The Present Kabalistic Tree of Life

(Note the separation between Malkuth and Tiphareth,
which reflects the split between mind and soul.)

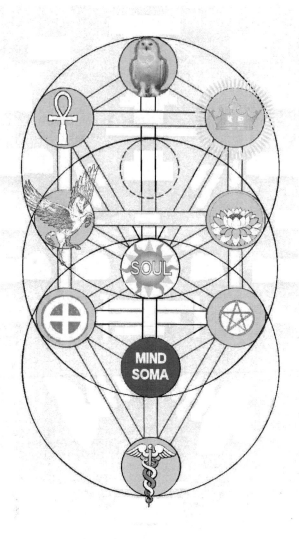

Fig. 14.3 The Aquarian Tree of Life
Showing the access symbols

(Note that with this Tree body, mind and soul are closely
united, yet still able to access the wisdom from the Sephiroth)

CHAPTER 15

Other Systems of Divination

O ver the course of time, many hundreds of different systems for accessing the psi quantum realm have been developed. Indeed, once the principles are understood, it would be very easy for you to invent your own methods, using either external objects or inner mental programs. Some of the exercises given in this book have been specially created for individuals coming to these concepts for the first time. New systems are being created all the time, as demonstrated by the proliferation of methods found in New Age shops. The traditional systems included in this book have been principally chosen because they are simple to use and do not require years of study to master. One of the other main systems of divination that you will come across is astrology, which deserves a mention although they will not be examined in detail as it is both quite complex and adequately covered in other books.

ASTROLOGY

Most people know the sign of the zodiac under which they were born and will probably recognize traits of character in themselves that reflect these signs. In this book, I have been suggesting that there are eight major focal points of energy or information in the quantum realm, which I have linked with different gods and goddesses, the I Ching, the Tarot and the runes. However, with astrology we are dealing with 12 principles, the 12 signs of the zodiac, so we need to consider this anomaly. The easiest way to reconcile this difference is to perceive that astrology reflects the harmonic resonance of the solar system as a whole, whereas the eightfold pattern connects more closely with the resonances of planet Earth. Another way of viewing this would be to perceive the energies from the eight quantum universities as if they were based on Earth, whereas the energies in astrology as if they came through the different planets and the signs of the zodiac, lying within this solar system. There is naturally an overlap between these two sets of forces, but the former allows for a positive interchange of information and energy, while the latter is a more passive, all-pervading influence that reflects the different rhythms of the whole solar system, as viewed from this planet.

There is naturally a close interchange between these two harmonics so it is quite possible to expand the eightfold pattern to its higher number if you so wish. This twelvefold pattern is also expressed in many other systems: the Chinese based their horoscope on a 12-yearly cycle, expressed through the characters of different animals, the rat, dog, boar and so on. This was expanded to 60 years through the five elements (5 x 12 = 60). The number five is perceived as the primary number of the human being in Chinese numerology, which was echoed by Leonardo da Vinci in his famous sketch of the proportions of a man. This is also why the five elements play such an integral part in acupuncture. The number 12 is found in the 12 apostles and the 12 knights of the Round Table.

CASTING AN ASTROLOGICAL CHART

To draw up an astrological chart, you will need to know accurately the day that you were born (e.g. 23 May 1948), the place in which you were born and the exact time at which you were born.

Today, most astrologers use computers to calculate a chart but I can remember having to work out all the information from astrological tables. Your chart is effectively a snapshot at the moment when you were born. It is this that is used to gain insight into the patterns and events that weave through your life, and particularly into aspects of your character.

TWIN STUDIES

Over the years, many studies have been carried out on identical and fraternal (or non-identical) twins to assess the differences in their character and life patterns. Some studies have been carried out on twins who have been separated at birth and adopted by different families. Despite this separation, a remarkable correlation was shown between identical twins with regard to the timing of different life events, family preferences and so on. For example, one set of twins, Jim Lewis and Jim Springer, who only met up when they were in their late thirties, had both divorced women called Linda and married second wives called Betty; had named their sons James Allan and James Alan; had each owned a dog called Toy and both used to spend their holidays on the same beach in Florida. These studies have also shown that identical twins have married on the same day, had accidents at the same time in their lives and experienced many other areas of synchronicity in their lives. Similar studies on fraternal twins have shown few of these similarities. It is true to say that no two twins are born at exactly the same time, and differences of a few minutes can change their respective astrological charts. Studies on twins have shown much higher instances of correlation between identical twins than fraternal ones, which could suggest that the genetic base is far more powerful than the astrological one in the creation of life patterns. Yet I believe that astrology can be placed in context by considering two points.

Firstly, within each person there is a different soul or spirit which will make that person unique. No two souls are exactly the same and, if one can accept the concept of reincarnation, then they would have had different lives. These prior experiences would shape their character and disposition in their present life. A good astrologer has to take into account these differences. Secondly, the astrological chart acts in exactly the same way as casting the I Ching or using the runes. In the final analysis it is the intuitive perception, or psi ability of astrologer, that will determine how good an assessment can be made; the greater the psi ability, the more accurate and beneficial the reading.

ASTROLOGY TODAY

Despite scientific advancements, astrology is more popular than ever. The sun sign predictions in the newspapers cannot be accurate, but they can sometimes make you think about aspects of your life that may need attention. Astrology is used in career assessments and personality readings. It can indicate likely trends and in this context is used by some analysts in predicting changes in shares and the stock market. This is controversial area, but I believe that a good astrologer is assessing the quantum realm, which has information on all these subjects.

There is not space here to cover all the uses of astrology adequately; however, there is one aspect of astrology that has wider relevance for predictive interpretations. This relates to the house system. In a full astrological chart, the position of the planets and the different astro-logical signs are set against 12 houses that express different ideas. For example, the ninth house relates to travel and higher education. A planet falling in that house would emphasize these aspects within the person's life. The sample astrological chart shown in Figure 15.1 illustrates this point.

The meanings of the 12 houses are as follows:

- **First house:** The self, appearances and the beginnings of new projects.
- **Second house:** Money, possessions, valuable objects, and support which will help a project grow.
- **Third house:** Communication, travel, siblings, education and day-to-day business matters.
- **Fourth house:** The family, home and the mother figure, conservation matters.
- **Fifth house:** Sport, pleasures, leisure activities, holidays, games, love affairs, creativity.
- **Sixth house:** Health, work, social responsibility.
- **Seventh house:** Relationships with others, marriage partnerships, agreements.
- **Eighth house:** Birth, death, transitions including beginnings and endings or projects. Sexuality, mysticism and interest in the paranormal.
- **Ninth house:** Travel, higher education, religion, law, freedom.

- **Tenth house:** Ambitions, aims, careers, status, self-worth and the father figure.
- **Eleventh house:** Friendships, clubs, societies, group projects, charities, hopes and wishes.
- **Twelfth house:** Psychology, dreams, hidden matters, the subconscious mind, anything below the surface, meditation, retreats and self-sacrifice.

Fig. 15.1

These houses are normally laid out in the way shown in Figure 15.1. An astrological chart is based on the position of the signs of the zodiac and the planets in these houses but we can equally place any other divinatory system, such as the runes, onto this chart. This will give another layer of meaning and allow you to gain a deeper or more extensive perception. An example exercise is given here using the runes, but any self-selective method such as the tarot, medicine cards or angel cards could be used. The symbol, rune or card would then be interpreted in line with the house in which it fell. For example, if the rune I (Isa), which means blockages or standstill, fell in the ninth house, then this would suggest travel delays, or educational impediments.

ASTROLOGICAL RUNE DIVINATION EXERCISE (time: 3 to 5 mins)

Aim: *To cast the runes into the twelve houses*

You will need a set of runes.

- Sit in one of the postures in Chapter 2 and close your eyes.
- Carry out the body awareness exercise in Chapter 2 and connect to your light within, then ask for a general life reading for this moment in time.
- Open your eyes and select one rune and place it on the table in front of you.
- Now select 12 runes and lay them out in accordance with Figure 15.2 so they resemble a clock face, but start with the rune at 9 o'clock and move back around in an anticlockwise direction (8 o'clock, 7 o'clock and so on).
- The rune in the middle controls the tenor of the whole reading.
- Now look up the meanings of the runes in relation to the position in which they fall and write down the answer for future reference.

Most of us would like to get positive encouragement and indications in all areas of our lives. In practice, this rarely occurs. Sometimes we need to accept that difficulties will emerge but we do not need to be fatalistic about what we get. All that these systems can do is give insight and, perhaps-more valuably, advance warning into the prevailing conditions that surround you. How you work that out is up to you. Let us suppose that you had set your heart on going to Australia at a particular time and the Isa rune came up, suggesting delays or impediments. It may be that this is not yet the right time to travel; reflect on what that might mean to you. Perhaps there is something that needs to be attended to first. If you still feel strongly about going at this time, make your booking but take all necessary precautions, such as travel insurance. In all these cases, you can also always ask for more insight and help, either by attuning within or drawing more runes.

Fig. 15.2 – Astrological Houses

Astrology has many uses, but it should not rule your life. Because the planets may seem to be in conflict in your chart on a particular day does not necessarily mean that everything will go wrong for you. We are all individual and influences that may be helpful to one can hinder another. If you use your intuition and common sense together, many useful insights will come your way.

OTHER SYSTEMS

There is an almost endless list of different divinatory systems, as any symbolic picture can be used to access the psi quantum realm. Some of the more popular systems today include crystal gazing or scrying, tea leaf reading, sand reading, crystal reading, Russian Fortune Telling Cards, Medicine Cards, Egyptian Cartouche cards and so on. Look out for different systems as you may come across one that really attracts you.

SECTION 4

POSITIVE USE OF PSYCHIC POWERS

CHAPTER 16

Manifesting Your Reality

As we have already seen, psi energy can flow in two directions; you can receive it and transmit it. In this section, we will focus on methods for directing psi energy to enhance your happiness, health, work and finances. There are many ways that individuals work with this concept, often at an unconscious level or, perhaps more accurately, without quite understanding why their 'positive' thoughts work. The most widely recognized use of directed psi energy is in psychic or spiritual healing. Many studies have also been carried out on cell cultures and seed germination, showing how the mind can interact and change some aspect of the physical environment.

Your thoughts and beliefs will shape your life. Change your thinking and the way that energy flows out from you will radically alter, modifying events in your environment. This is an exciting prospect and in this section we will focus on methods that can make this a positive reality in your life.

GOALS AND LIFE PLANS

Each soul, when it comes into a physical body, has a sense of what it wishes to achieve during that life. This is a self-determined choice and not one imposed by some all-powerful deity. However, misdeeds in one life can get carried through to the next in that some form of atonement needs to be made. This can be achieved in many different ways and some souls will deliberately choose a hard life, perhaps one filled with suffering, as part of this atonement process. Even so, your future is not fixed but is constantly being created. At any moment you can change the way you are, through some inner realization, and that will immediately affect your future. Our lives are not predestined and never will be. It is the intentions of the soul that are paramount, and it is this that sets the pattern of our lives.

An important choice had to be made, before your conception, on the type of family that you would be born into. The consequences of that choice set up a powerful impulse that has played an important part in shaping your life. Yet neither your upbringing nor your genetic makeup need be deterrents to leading a happy, fulfilled life. If you do not feel fulfilled, it is important to explore why and how you are blocking this aspect within yourself. By learning to work creatively with the energies from the quantum realm, you can change the dynamics of your life pattern and move towards realizing your full potential.

SETTING OBJECTIVES

Before you can begin changing your life pattern by setting new objectives, it is important to take stock of where you are at the moment. You cannot build a new future and set new goals unless you have made a clear assessment of your present position. One way to do this is by making an assessment of how the eight archetypal principles are manifested within you, using the following questionnaire. You might like to write the questions down on a piece of paper so that you can fill it in and add any comments as you go along. Mark your response with a circle on a scale of 1 to 8 where 1 is very unsatisfactory or unfulfilled and 8 is very satisfactory or fulfilled. It is important that you are honest with yourself in answering the questions.

1. INITIATION:

	Unsatisfactory				Satisfactory			
Spiritual expression	1.	2.	3.	4.	5.	6.	7.	8.
Ability to accept authority	1.	2.	3.	4.	5.	6.	7.	8.
Ability to be in authority	1.	2.	3.	4.	5.	6.	7.	8.
Ability to be broad-minded	1.	2.	3.	4.	5.	6.	7.	8.
Ability to accept yourself	1.	2.	3.	4.	5.	6.	7.	8.
Ability to start new projects	1.	2.	3.	4.	5.	6.	7.	8.

2. TRANSFORMATION:

Ability to change	1.	2.	3.	4.	5.	6.	7.	8.
Ability to cope with fear	1.	2.	3.	4.	5.	6.	7.	8.
Ability to be courageous	1.	2.	3.	4.	5.	6.	7.	8.

3. EXPLORATION:

Making new discoveries	1.	2.	3.	4.	5.	6.	7.	8.
Ability to have fun	1.	2.	3.	4.	5.	6.	7.	8.
Ability to be childlike	1.	2.	3.	4.	5.	6.	7.	8.
Ability to explore within	1.	2.	3.	4.	5.	6.	7.	8.
Ability to be loyal	1.	2.	3.	4.	5.	6.	7.	8.

4. FORMATION:

Ability to handle money	1.	2.	3.	4.	5.	6.	7.	8.
Ability to have your needs met	1.	2.	3.	4.	5.	6.	7.	8.
Career / work fulfillment	1.	2.	3.	4.	5.	6.	7.	8.
Ability to ground new projects	1.	2.	3.	4.	5.	6.	7.	8.
Ability to express creative ideas	1.	2.	3.	4.	5.	6.	7.	8.
Ability to complete tasks	1.	2.	3.	4.	5.	6.	7.	8.
Ability to be generous	1.	2.	3.	4.	5.	6.	7.	8.

5. COMMUNICATION:

Ability to speak in public	1.	2.	3.	4.	5.	6.	7.	8.
Ability to share ideas with others	1.	2.	3.	4.	5.	6.	7.	8.
Enjoy writing letters	1.	2.	3.	4.	5.	6.	7.	8.
Ability to learn	1.	2.	3.	4.	5.	6.	7.	8.
Travelling	1.	2.	3.	4.	5.	6.	7.	8.
Ability to be trustworthy	1.	2.	3.	4.	5.	6.	7.	8.
Health	1.	2.	3.	4.	5.	6.	7.	8.

6. ORGANISATION:

Close friendships	1.	2.	3.	4.	5.	6.	7.	8.
Sex life	1.	2.	3.	4.	5.	6.	7.	8.
Emotional relationships	1.	2.	3.	4.	5.	6.	7.	8.
Ability to organize your life	1.	2.	3.	4.	5.	6.	7.	8.
Ability to empathize	1.	2.	3.	4.	5.	6.	7.	8.
Ability to share feelings	1.	2.	3.	4.	5.	6.	7.	8.
Co-operation with others	1.	2.	3.	4.	5.	6.	7.	8.
Ability to be forgiving	1.	2.	3.	4.	5.	6.	7.	8.
Home environment	1.	2.	3.	4.	5.	6.	7.	8.
Work environment	1.	2.	3.	4.	5.	6.	7.	8.

7. REFLECTION:

Recreational activities	1.	2.	3.	4.	5.	6.	7.	8.
Time for quiet	1.	2.	3.	4.	5.	6.	7.	8.
Ability to meditate	1.	2.	3.	4.	5.	6.	7.	8.
Being at peace with oneself	1.	2.	3.	4.	5.	6.	7.	8.
Sleep patterns	1.	2.	3.	4.	5.	6.	7.	8.

8. INNOVATION:

Ability to have creative ideas	1.	2.	3.	4.	5.	6.	7.	8.
Being individualistic	1.	2.	3.	4.	5.	6.	7.	8.
Enjoyment of life	1.	2.	3.	4.	5.	6.	7.	8.
Ability to stand by your beliefs	1.	2.	3.	4.	5.	6.	7.	8.
Ability to plan for the future	1.	2.	3.	4.	5.	6.	7.	8.
Weight	1.	2.	3.	4.	5.	6.	7.	8.

When you have completed this questionnaire, look closely at what has emerged, particularly where you have circled numbers 1, 2, 7 or 8. Do any patterns emerge? Do you feel you are strong or weak in any of these archetypal areas?

There may be some aspects which have not been included are important facets in your life. If so, try to allocate them to categories and assess them on a 1 to 8 basis.

SETTING NEW GOALS

Select three aspects from the list that you would like to change. It does not matter whether they come from three different categories or are all in the same group. Then describe, in one sentence each: where you are now with the problem; and where you would like to be in the future. You will need to do this for each of the three areas that you wish to change. When you have done this look closely at the three areas, then select the one that you most wish to change. Now carry out the following exercise:

GOAL SETTING EXERCISE (time: 3 to 5 mins)

Aim: *To set new goals in your life*

- Sit in one of the postures in Chapter 2 and close your eyes.
- Carry out the body awareness exercise in Chapter 2 and connect to your inner light.
- Make a connection to the Sun (center of wheel) by imagining that a golden thread of light connects you to this source of power and initiatory action.
- Affirm within that you wish to change the dynamic of the particular situation that has been bothering you and ask that you are given the power and courage to change what needs to be changed.
- Observe whether you think or are aware of any inner blockages that might prevent this happening.
- Now think of your new objective and visualize or sense this coming into your life and feel the sun's energy empowering your new concept.
- Send a thought of thanks back to the Sun and then bring yourself back to full waking consciousness.

This exercise should be repeated at least three times until the changes that you have initiated start to become manifest in your life. During this process, note any other changes that are taking place as all aspects of our consciousness are inter-linked.

LINGUISTIC PROGRAMMING

So many patterns become ingrained in our consciousness through the words that we use, and the inner messages that we continually give ourselves. For example, the word 'can't' is often used when there is no physical limitation to what can be achieved. As soon as you use the word 'can't or 'could never', you immediately limit your potential. I have helped many people to reverse attitudes that have become ingrained within them by the repetition of the language that they use.

Nobody is perfect and we all have something to learn and discover. It may be very valid to acknowledge that there are some things in our lives that we find difficult. I know that there are quite a number in mine. But that is very different from saying that you 'can't' do something. Look closely at all the negative comments that you make about yourself and then think about what you can change. Words carry power. When you make detrimental statements about yourself, you reinforce your negative beliefs.

Most importantly, you must believe that there is nothing that you cannot change or bring into your life. Belief is all-important. As soon as you believe that you can achieve some change, you will unconsciously make connections to the energy from the quantum realm to make this a part of your reality. Not only are the universities of the quantum realm sources of knowledge, they are also sources of power. By learning to link consciously with these energies, you will speed up the manifestation of events in your life. What you set your heart upon can become your reality, with only one or two provisos. These are, however, very important.

Firstly, you cannot set in motion anything that might harm another, or influence them to do something against their will. If you try to do this, you will certainly get a kickback sooner or later, as any misuse of energy is self-destructive. If, for example, you fancy having a sexual relationship with a particular person, knowing inwardly that such a relationship would be inappropriate, and you try to visualize it happening, it will never be fruitful. In all relationship situations you must only ever offer up your thoughts on the basis that what is right for the other person must also be allowed to be manifest. On the other hand, if you feel that someone is adversely dominating you, then you have every right to break that link. You can call upon as much help as you can muster to sever any chains of dominance, for no-one has the right to inflict their power on another in a detrimental way.

Secondly, although material possessions are an important part of physical existence they are not everything. There are many very unhappy and unfulfilled rich people. There is nothing wrong with having more possessions but they should not be seen as ends in themselves. The key to life is finding out what you really love doing and then directing that activity into some process that benefits others. Any activity, trade, profession or business can fall into this category and appropriate financial reward can be part of that. Life is to be enjoyed, not endured. If you are in a career that you dislike, then call upon the help of the quantum realm. Miracles can happen if you allow them into your life.

ACHIEVING YOUR OBJECTIVES - THE DYNAMICS OF MONEY

Money reflects the energy of exchange, which is a fundamental requirement of all life. All species are sustained by the energy of the sun, either directly or indirectly, and are able to survive by exchanging energy between them. It is the sun's energy that plants use to grow; they then provide us and other creatures with energy in the form of food. Money is a convenient way of quantifying this energy exchange in the human domain. Unfortunately there has been a down-side. The acquisition of money is often seen as synonymous with a person's status or real worth and it has also tended to foster an attitude of greed. It can generate feelings of resentment and jealousy against those who have acquired wealth. All these emotions can be difficult to handle, giving money some of its unfortunate connotations. However, we should not forget that it is not money itself which causes these problems but us. Therefore, it is our attitudes to money and the way in which money acts as a symbol for other issues that are important.

For example, if you equate money with self-worth, a lack of it can be an inner way of you affirming your worthlessness, that somehow you are undeserving. It is therefore important to explore your attitudes to money and the way in which those attitudes shape your existence. It is always important to ask how much more money would change your life. Would the money itself really make you happier? Money, seen as 'energy', also needs to flow. I think that those who have found real happiness with their wealth have been as happy using it to support deserving causes as they have been in making it. Block the exchange of energy one way or the other, and sooner or later problems will arise which will often come out in other areas of your life.

Patterns in life also tend to flow between highs and lows. There are many individuals who have made a fortune, lost it, and then made a fortune again. One of the key elements is not to give up believing that you can achieve what you wish. Set your goals, then visualize them coming into being.

In working with the energy of money, it is much better thinking about what it is that you wish to achieve rather than the money itself. Let us suppose that you wished to start your own business and that this would require £50,000. Instead of visualizing the money coming to you, focus on the business and see yourself achieving your objectives. To assist this process you will need to call upon the energy from the Yellow university. To do this, carry out the following exercise.

It is important that you have some clarity on your objectives (clarity is one of the determining qualities of the Yellow university). For example, if you need a car, visualize the sort of car that you would like, and then offer it out to the cosmos; it is important that once you have sent out your image you allow the cosmos to shape it into its most appropriate form. On one occasion, while looking to establish a particular project, I had a very clear idea of how it should be manifest. However, the cosmos knew better, and what finally emerged was far more appropriate and far-reaching than I had initially intended.

ACHIEVING YOUR OBJECTIVES EXERCISE (time: 5 to 10 mins)

Aim: To assist the development of any projects

- Clearly write down what you wish to achieve, possess or require.
- Your will need to link with the energy from the Yellow university and the symbol for this is a golden coin inscribed with a pentangle.
- Sit in one of the postures in Chapter 2 and close your eyes.
- Carry out the body awareness exercise in Chapter 2 and connect to your inner light.
- Link into the energy of the Yellow university by sensing or visualizing its color around you and also imagine a link with the golden coin.
- Now think of your project and visualize that whatever you wish to materialize is occurring.
- Send out the thought that it can happen in whatever way is most appropriate.
- Now offer up the image that you have created into the sun and de-link from the energy of the Yellow university.
- Finally, send out a thought of thanks for the help received and bring yourself back to full conscious reality.

WORKING ON OTHER AREAS OF YOUR LIFE

The process described above can be used in any area of your life. Select the most appropriate university and then call upon the energy from it to help you. Indeed, you may need to obtain help from a number of different universities for a particular project. A recent book that I was writing needed quite a bit of research which came under the Orange university. Help came in all sorts of unexpected ways, through individuals, newspaper articles which exactly described an aspect of the topic and so on. The actual writing was inspired by the energy of the Green university, with additional help from the others when needed. As I have said before, all that is necessary is to plug into this other dimension and it will help you enormously. You can do this on a daily basis if you like. Just believe and your life may well be transformed.

CHAPTER 17

The Power to Heal

The power to heal is a natural gift that we all possess. Like all gifts, it can be enhanced by training and practice and particularly by understanding its principles. Healing can be directed to any situation where imbalance occurs, including physical, emotional, mental and spiritual ailments, as well as relationships between people. It can range from sending energy to help someone recover from a physical injury, to the powerful miracles of Christ. Its potential uses are endless, but for most people it is generally of great value in helping illnesses within the family or friends or with relationship problems at work. There will be a time in your life when an ability to bring healing energy to a person will help their recovery. You can call upon this same energy for self-healing whenever you are sick or suffering from a particular problem. Developing this gift is rather like learning first aid. You never know when it will be necessary, but when a situation arises your ability to help may be life-saving. The exciting thing is that the more that you learn to use this part of you, the more you will recognize its potential benefits. It is a gift that I use extensively to support members of my own family and I am of the firm opinion that it has made a considerable difference to their lives.

Healing is no longer a hypothetical concept, but has been subjected to rigorous tests in laboratory conditions. These have demonstrated the mind's ability to influence cell cultures, plant growth and speed up seed germination. Such tests have been regularly repeated by individuals who claim a healing gift. Not so easy to assess are the studies on human beings, for here many other factors come into play. However, the successful double-blind study carried out by Dr Randolph Byrd from the USA, described in Chapter 1, strongly supports the idea that we all possess healing ability.

There are many people in some form of therapeutic practice where the ability to use their healing gift consciously would greatly enhance the effectiveness of their treatments. Dr Larry Dossey, the author of *Healing Words*, has suggested that in the not too distant future, every patient admitted to hospital would automatically be given healing as part of their treatment. This is an exciting prospect.

The practice of healing at a basic level is very simple, involving no more than the projection of positive thoughts to another. It does not involve any complicated rituals or require a special attitude of mind but can be readily incorporated into your life. It is true to say that some people have greater aptitude than others, as in essence it is akin to any artistic skill. Just as some individuals have reached the heights of musical attainment, so there are some healers who have devoted their whole lives to practicing their gift. Yet, as most people are able to express some aspect of musical skill, so you can express your healing ability if you so choose.

There is no one way to heal, and it could be said that there are as many different techniques as there are healers. Discovering how you can best express this gift is an important part of the process. There are, however, a few practical considerations, and in this chapter I will give you ample information to set you on the path of unlocking your healing skills. Techniques will be suggested, as these can be helpful for the novice. These should be looked upon as stepping-stones; once the concepts have been mastered, you can go on exploring the many different ways of directing your healing energy. The more that I have tapped these skills within me, the more I realize how little I know. Developing new insights adds excitement and interest in the exploration of who and what we are.

THE HEALING GIFT

There exists within you an incredible healing power which springs into action as soon as your equilibrium is disturbed. You do not have to tell your white blood cells to attack any foreign bodies when you cut yourself, or inform your body that it requires repair. Any damage is rectified very quickly and, in the vast majority of cases, without any additional support. One way of looking at healing is to consider that a healer is someone who is able to access their own healing power and project this out to another when they need help.

We have already discussed how energy is transferred between individuals. Simply thinking of someone opens up the potential for energy to be transferred. One of the important skills in healing is being able to create sufficient rapport with the recipient for energy to flow across a reasonable number of frequencies. Energy will be exchanged when similar parts are resonating together or are on the same wavelength. Your radio at home will only pick up a broadcasting station if it is able to tune into the correct frequency. The margin of error is very small, as slight changes on the dial will distort and then remove the signal altogether. In the same way, as a healer, you will need to be able to adjust your signal to that of your patient for your healing energy to be transferred.

This may sound complicated but in practice it is very simple, occurring at a subconscious level. The most important quality is your desire to help and your willingness to make such a connection. A sick person will generally be in an energetically depleted state so that your energy can be easily transferred into them. There are some exceptions to this rule which will be covered later.

TIREDNESS AND EXHAUSTION

When a person becomes sick, their ability to recharge their energy can become impaired. They will also require a considerable amount of energy to carry out any repair processes. Healing then, at its most basic level, can be directed to providing additional energy to another for their recovery. However, discharging some of your energy in this way will cause your reservoir of energy to become depleted. Let us suppose that you needed to give healing to several people (four has been shown to be the limit): without recharging, you would soon end up with flat batteries. This type of energy discharge can sometimes occur unconsciously. Many people have had the experience of being with an elderly person and suddenly, for no apparent reason, starting to feel completely exhausted. I believe that what is happening here is a leaching of energy.

Healers wrestling with this problem in the past discovered that they could overcome this impediment in a very simple way. Instead of using their own energy, they plugged into an outside source. In this way, they acted as a channel for healing energy rather than drawing upon their own reserves. If you can develop this system satisfactorily, there is no reason why you could not give healing to 20 people in a row without any feelings of exhaustion. Indeed, understanding and using this principle is one of the keys to vitality. Any interaction that you have with one another will cause energy to be expended. If you are using only your own reserves, you will end-up becoming exhausted. There are many professions, such as teaching and nursing, where this can be an acute problem. Learning to plug into an outside source of energy, drawing upon that for your supply, will go a long way to relieving fatigue.

I once discussed this problem with Nicholas Daniel, a well-known concert musician, who happened to remark that it was only when he looked to drawing energy from outside himself that his performances really took off and he would finish feeling as energized or even more energized than before he began. Before he discovered this principle, he would finish a performance feeling totally drained.

ENERGY RESERVOIRS

As you might guess, the main reservoirs of energy available to us stem from the eight universities of the quantum realm. By plugging into the relevant source, you can channel a limitless supply of energy through your system. You will never deplete the reserves of energy that are available to you. Your only limitation is the amplitude of energy that you can channel, for your system is rather like a fuse which will only take so much energy before blowing. Someone who has trained themselves in healing will be able to channel a stronger or more powerful level of energy. It is no different in essence from an athlete training to run faster or jump higher.

In channeling energy through you in this way, you can bring different flavors to bear according to the situation. Someone who was very agitated or mentally distraught, for example, would probably require the energy from the Indigo university, which carries a feeling of calm and peace. One of the most powerful of the healing energies stems from the Blue university, which carries the qualities of love and forgiveness. There is an exercise on the next page from my book, *The Healer Within.*

You might like to write down your answers to the visualization exercise, as it can be helpful to retain information about your progress. This exercise can be used as a model for all healing activity. As already stated each of the universities has a role to play in the healing process. An overview of their functions is:

- 1. **Magenta:** General healing and vitality and back problems, which often reflect a feeling of lack of support on a psychological level. Also spiritual problems and the connections with the inner core of our being. This is one of the important protective energies.
- 2. **Red:** Transformation and change on a psychological level. This is an ideal university to connect with if you are engaged in psychotherapy. It is also helpful with physically conditions where there is an excess of fluids such as ulcers.
- 3. **Orange:** Psychological problems that are buried in the psyche from the past. This energy will help bring them to the surface. Also helps in confronting the shadowy side of our nature, particularly our fears.
- 4. **Yellow:** Physical eye problems, and lack of direction at a psychological level.
- 5. **Green:** General energy balancing. Integrating the Yin/Yang (anima/animus) aspects of our being. Past life and karmic problems.
- 6. **Blue:** Its protective and harmonizing quality make this one of the best all-round energies for healing. Also helps with forgiveness and letting go of past resentments which are always self-destructive.
- 7. **Indigo:** Situations that require peace and calm, including mental conditions, hyperactivity and so on. Alcohol and drug abuse can also be helped by this energy.
- 8. **Violet:** Protection from negative influences, depression and anxiety. This is an excellent energy for general recharging when feeling physically or mentally depleted.

BASIC HEALING EXERCISE (time: 5 to 10 mins)

Aim: To project healing energy

- Sit in one of the postures in Chapter 2 and close your eyes.
- Carry out the body awareness exercise in Chapter 2 and connect to your inner light.
- Think of the quality of 'love'. What does it mean to you? Now, by visualizing, try to answer the following questions:
  - Which color do I associate with 'love'?
  - Where would I locate this quality within my body?
  - What animal do I associate with 'love' and where is that animal in relation to me?
  - What flower do I associate with 'love'?
  - What item of clothing do I associate with 'love' and what do I feel when I wear this in my imagination?
- Next imagine that you are linking yourself to the power of the Blue university, by either sensing yourself surrounded by a blue light, or linking to the symbol of the Ankh.
- Now think of a person who is very dear to you and project a thought of love towards them.
- Next think of someone who needs help and send them a thought of love.
- Now think of someone whom you don't get on with and send them a thought of love.
- Finally, send yourself a thought of love, thinking particularly of those aspects that you dislike about yourself.
- When you have finished bring yourself back to waking consciousness and open your eyes.

In drawing the energy from these different sources of power, you only have to link your mind to their color or symbol; either approach will do. You can then experiment with these different rays to see which ones come easily to you and the effects that they have.

If you feel uncomfortable with this idea, I believe that it is valid to ask for God's help or that of an individual such as Christ. Many great teachers have reflected one or other of these universities and part of the reasons for their incarnation has been to ground these energies down from the spiritual plane. Christ, for example, I would link with the Magenta university, whereas Buddha sits in the Indigo. Another alternative source of energy is the earth itself and I know a number of people who will link with this energy by drawing it up through their feet.

HEALTH AND DISEASE

For you to be healthy there needs to be a balanced flow of energy between the different layers of your being. We have discussed how these can be divided into four broad categories: physical, emotion, mental and spiritual. These four layers have sometimes been subdivided.

Energy within us flows in the same way that sound moves across the notes of a piano. As soon as any one note is played a vibration is set up in the string which immediately causes all other notes on the same octave (frequency) to vibrate. By playing middle C on the piano every other C note will vibrate providing they are in tune. If not, a distortion in the sound will occur. I am sure most of you will have heard how unpleasant an out-of-tune piano can be. In the same way within us, if any part is not in harmony with the rest, breakdowns occur, leading to disease. There is a symphony of sound playing within us all the time; restore your inner harmony and health will immediately follow.

To achieve this, energy is required and one of the simplest ways is by providing extra energy for the person who needs help. However, if we look a little more closely at the piano analogy some additional insights emerge.

A piano may not work or be out of tune for a number of reasons. Someone, as I once did as a child, might have spilt condensed milk over the keyboard causing the keys to stick. The temperature in the room may have changed, causing the strings to come slightly off tune, or something might have landed on the piano, damaging its structure. Correcting each of these situations necessitates a slightly different approach. In the first case, we need to remove the offending substance and clean up the piano to restore it to full working order. In the second, slight adjustments to the key tuners will be all that is called for and in the third, extensive repairs will be necessary. From this, you will see that there are fundamentally three different approaches you can take. You can:

- Remove unwanted energy.
- Balance what is already there.
- Put new energy into the system.

These three approaches should be considered when you are giving healing, which are expanded as described below in the order that they might be approached in a healing situation.

BALANCING ENERGY

The most important aspect of all healing is balance. Nothing on the physical level is in perfect balance, but without balance we believe that the universe would fall apart and all life would cease to exist. Whatever the situation, you can always send a thought of balance to it, by visualizing a balancing symbol, connecting to the right university or simply affirming inwardly the words "I am of balanced". The Green university with its symbol of the caduceus or the Violet university with its symbol of the equidistant cross within a circle are perhaps the best ones to use. Projecting the images of these symbols to the client or patient will bring forth a quality of balance.

CLEANSING ENERGY

We can all accumulate unwanted energies from time to time, of which I believe that viral or bacterial infections are but a physical symptom. Such energies need to be cleansed from the system. The most appropriate energy to do this comes from the Blue university and using this color is perhaps the most effective way of achieving this objective. You can imagine that a blue light is washing through the person's energy fields and discharging any unwanted substances back into the earth.

RECHARGING ENERGY

The most effective recharging energies stem from the Magenta university, symbolized by the sun's rays. By imagining that you are surrounding a person in sunlight you will do much to restore their vitality and optimism. A good alternative is drawing on the synthesis of all the universities through the color white. In this case, you can either surround them with this color, or direct this energy to their solar plexus if they are physically tired, or to their head if mentally run down.

THE DYNAMICS OF LIFE

In Chinese medicine, health was perceived as a balance between three different qualities of energy known as Ch'i, Shen and Jing. Ch'i is the energy from the environment and is drawn into us by the food we eat, the liquids that we drink and the air that we breathe. It also covers all the levels of energy which stem from the eight universities. Jing relates to sexual energy as well as to the forces from our genetic inheritance. It relates to our ancestral patterns and to those conditions that come directly from our forebears. Shen is the energy from our spiritual self and includes karmic patterns stemming from past lives and all previous experiences.

In western terms, Ch'i or environmental influences and Jing, genetic patterning, is well understood in the nature/nurture debates that have swung back and forth over the past 150 years. Western medicine and science misses out the third leg of the triangle, to its detriment, I think. All three need to be in broad balance for health to be maintained. Illness can stem from any one of these legs and healing may be required to be focused on one or other of these areas to restore equilibrium.

Many people today use orthodox medicine and psychotherapy to cover environmental, emotional and psychological problems, which are generally the most common ailments. Spiritual difficulties, once the sole domain of the priesthood, are now also helped by past life or soul therapies. Ancestral problems do not at present get as much attention as they should, but my courses and book, *Healing Your Ancestral Patterns*, cover this field.

FINDING BALANCE

For full health, we need to find a balance between all these different aspects of our being. As I have discussed, we each possess a powerful self-regulating energy which generally works well without too many problems. Like all machines, it requires attention, in the form of the type of foods we eat and how we conduct our lives. Create too much stress and problems are bound to manifest themselves. You can always tell how balanced you are by looking at ALL the facets of your life, not just your health. If you completed the questionnaire in Chapter 16, you will have a very good idea of the areas that need attention. I believe that we do not normally suffer physical ill-health unless there is a contributory reason coming from a deeper level within the psyche. In this sense, all disease has a psychosomatic element. As long as you pay attention to what is going on in your life and tackle situations as they emerge, you will be able to maintain your health and vitality into old age. However, we all have to die sometime. This is perhaps the one certainty of life. I think that death is but the shedding of the physical body and that the inner part of you will continue to exist on another level of consciousness. The near death experiences described earlier show how easy it is for a person's consciousness or inner being to separate from their body and to experience powerfully things in another dimension. This is a natural part of life and I believe that the time and method of your passing will generally be your choice. I qualify this as the wonders of modern medicine have sometimes interfered with this process. Do not be sad for someone close to death, as they will almost certainly be much happier where they are going to than those who are left behind. It is natural to grieve for those who leave us, but try to see this in the same way that you would if they had emigrated to a foreign country. I believe that you will always be connected and sooner or later you will meet up again - of that you can be assured.

Developing Your Healing Potential

ATTITUDES AND HEALING

Before you embark on healing others, there are a few other considerations. Firstly, healing should never be an imposition, only an offering. In learning to harness your thoughts and direct energy, you can do much to help all sorts of situations around you. But, like all energy, this gift can also be misused. There are, as we have discussed, balancing mechanisms in the cosmos that ensure that sooner or later we have to pick up the tab for that which we have given out. In this sense, nobody is above the law, so it is important that you use your thoughts and abilities in a beneficial way.

One of the traps that is easy to fall into is thinking that you know better than the person you are trying to help. There are a few situations where this may be true. All children need firm but gentle handling and there are times when we have to insist on something, such as when we take them to school for the first time. But carrying this attitude into adulthood is a very different thing. At best, it requires a very high level of sensitivity and spiritual awareness; at worst it is pure arrogance. The only person who can really judge what is right for a particular soul in incarnation is themselves. So, as a healer, it is very important that you do not try to subject your patients to the dictates of your beliefs. This raises the question of whether we are imposing our will over another by sending them healing? The answer to that is no, with the proviso that you first perceive their acceptance to receiving your help. Some people will only send healing to those who have directly asked for it, and that is one way around the situation. But there is another way.

Before sending healing to another person it is important that you first connect with them on a mental level and then send a thought that your healing is a freely offered gift to them. Some people like to make the inner affirmation, 'Thy will be done'. If you do this, you will never infringe the inner wishes of their soul and the healing will only be of benefit. Their higher wisdom will be able to use your healing energy in the way that is most appropriate for what they wish to achieve.

This can be a particular problem when a friend, colleague or family member is facing a life-threatening illness. It is quite natural for everybody to wish that person makes a full recovery. The medical profession and therapists can also believe that the death of a patient is a sign of their failure. It is not, and never has been. In fact, keeping a person alive at all costs can be a much greater failure than letting them die peacefully. In offering healing to people in these situations, it is most important that you do so in an open, non-controlling way. By all means focus your healing on helping them recover, but also acknowledge that they can use this same energy if they so wish to help with their passing. This can be hard to accept by the therapist or family member but from the soul's point of view it is most important.

WHEN NOT TO HEAL

There are two types of situations when healing should not be given. The first involves you, the healer.

Healing can only occur when there is a reasonable level of resonance between you and the person you are directing your energies towards. To do this, you need to be in a general state of good health yourself. You should not send healing if you have any bacteriological or viral infections or are experiencing any severe mental or emotional turmoil. Nobody is perfect, so in that sense we all have levels of imbalance within us. Indeed, by sending healing to another you will actually help highlight and correct many imbalances within you. It is, however, also important that you take a responsible attitude and do not try to direct healing energies to others if you are seriously suffering in any way. In such situations it is much better to call upon those higher energies to help you.

In the second situation, there are some conditions that require specialist help and should not be tackled unless you have had considerable experience. These include all severe mental or psychotic conditions including schizophrenia and true possession cases. There is not space here to cover these situations adequately but sometimes individuals in these states hold very powerful destructive energies around them. If you try to tackle them this destructive energy can flow into you. The rule here is, 'In doubt, do nowt.'

HEALING TECHNIQUES

To begin with, most people, often through embarrassment, prefer to send distant healing rather than face a person on a one-to-one basis. The methods given here cover both eventualities.

There is one other point that needs to be mentioned before you begin. Studies carried out in the USA suggest that healing is much more successful when directed to the whole person rather than focusing upon a specific part of them. What does this mean in practice? Let us suppose that someone suffering from an arthritic knee asks for healing. You could send your healing to them as a person without thinking of the knee at all, or you could just focus on healing the knee. The former method works the best so that should always be uppermost when sending out any healing. The system given here incorporates both elements so you will be well covered if you adopt this method.

Suggested Healing Procedure

- Connect to your inner light.
- Attune to the client and their inner light, wherever you sense it to be.
- Link to your source of healing energy, e.g. sun, blue light, golden chalice, Christ, God or the earth.
- Direct your thoughts towards balancing the whole energy field of your client.
- Send healing to any specific areas, e.g. an arthritic knee.
- Balance the whole person once again.
- De-link from your source of energy and from the client.
- Sense yourself centered and balanced within and close down.

Let us look at these stages in a little more detail.

When attuning within, you can carry out the procedure on how to connect to your inner light in Chapter 2. It is important that you give time to sensing the connection to the core part of yourself. When you attune to your client, imagine that they also have an inner light which reflects their spiritual self. Sense that you are linking your light with theirs. This will allow a harmonizing process to occur between you. Remember to acknowledge that it is an offering of healing that you are giving them, not an imposition.

To link with your source of healing energy, visualize or sense that a connection is being made through the color or symbol you have chosen and draw that energy, either down through the top of your head or up through your feet. You will get a slightly different flavor from each approach but both are valid. For example, if you wished to use the sun as a source of Ch'i, you could imagine that a golden beam of sunlight was entering through the top of your head before being channeled to the client.

The simplest way to send healing to the whole person is to see them surrounded in a sphere of light that is balancing all aspects of their being. A light blue is a good general color to use. When sending healing to the specific part, hold your hands close to or over the affected area, without actually touching them. Sense the energy coming through your hands and correcting the imbalances, whatever they might be. When sending distant healing, you will need to imagine or visualize that an energy beam of light is focusing onto the location of the problem. For example, if a subject suffers from a heart condition, having first sent healing to the whole person you could imagine that the healing energy is gently flowing into the area surrounding their heart. Allow your intuition to guide your actions and remember that physical conditions will, in general, also have an emotional or mental element. Healing can also be sent to those other aspects of the self.

In step 6, repeat step 4, sensing that all aspects are being balanced within the individual. Normally, I will also send an extra thought to strengthen the subject's aura at this stage.

In step 7, it is important that you disconnect both from the client and your source before completing the healing. Failure to do this will result in you continuing to be drawn upon by the client. It is also important to disconnect from the source of the healing energy because the link that you made to it was set up especially for that particular situation. Its energies will be right for the patient but not necessarily for you.

Finally, spend a few moments sensing the balance of energy within yourself, and try to feel that every part of you is whole and integrated.

These eight steps are a simple guide that will allow you to start expressing your individual healing ability. To enhance your skills, you may wish to attend a healing course (details are given in the appendix).

HOW TO GIVE HEALING

When you are giving direct healing to a person, it is preferable to have them either sitting in a straight chair or lying on the floor or couch. As the healer, you need to be in a position that is comfortable for you. If possible, place your hands on their shoulders before starting. This may not always be possible, say, if you were giving healing to someone in a hospital bed. However, touch is very important and creates an initial bond; holding a person's hand can be just as effective. After your initial physical contact, it is normally better to work with your hands 4 to 18 inches from the client's body. With direct touch, there is a greater tendency for your own energies to leak out into the patient, which is not desirable.

Many novice healers feel self-conscious when they begin, but with practice this will cease to be a problem. You will sense the healing energy flowing through your hands, through a tingling sensation or sometimes heat. This energy can then be directed quite naturally, as appropriate. When you have finished it is always good to send out a thought of thanks for help that you have received.

When sending distant healing to a person, imagine or sense that they are sitting in front of you. You do not have to visualize them in great detail for the healing to be effective. Just feeling that they are before you will suffice. When you have finished, sense or imagine that you are lifting them up into the light and carry out your normal disconnection exercises. You will then feel you are free to go on to the next case.

Below is a simple distant healing exercise that you can safely use. You will need to think of someone who needs help or healing. It could be a friend or member of your family or, indeed, an animal.

DISTANT HEALING EXERCISE (time: 15 mins)

Aim: *To send healing to another person*

- Sit in one of the postures in Chapter 2 and close your eyes.
- Carry out the body awareness exercise in Chapter 2 and connect to your inner light.
- Imagine or sense the person that you are going to send healing to is sitting in front of you.
- Sense that you are connecting to their inner light, imagining that you are linking the light within you to the light within them by a golden thread. Affirm inwardly the words, 'Thy will be done'.
- Connect to your source of healing energy and feel it flowing down through the top of your head, or up through your feet as you prefer. Then direct that energy through your hands to the person. With practice, this will become a continual process, rather like turning on a tap and knowing that as long as it is open the water will flow.
- Sense or hold the thought in your mind that this energy is balancing the whole person. To make this more real, you could imagine an equidistant cross is superimposed over them. Hold the thought until you sense they are balanced.
- Allow your imagination to prompt you to any other aspect that needs healing in a specific way. For example, if you know that they have a damaged ankle, focus the healing energy there. Return to sending healing once more to the whole person, but this time imagine that they are surrounded in a bubble of light.
- Disconnect the golden light that you held between you, and disconnect also from the source of energy that is flowing through you.
- Sit for a moment balancing your own energies before opening your eyes.

If you wish, you can then write down your experiences. Some healers also like to wash their hands after each case and this too can be a useful discipline, symbolizing the de-linking of energy from the patient.

How Long Should I Give Healing For?

There are no hard and fast rules on this. I have met some healers who will send healing for nearly an hour and others, like the Russian healer Barbara Ivanova, who focus for barely half a minute. Christ's cures were often reported to be instantaneous. In my own case, I will normally give healing for as long as I can hold the focus of my attention on what I am doing. This is generally 5 to 10 minutes.

SELF-HEALING

Self-healing falls into two categories: maintenance and dealing with specific imbalances.

We all need help from time to time, whether it be from a doctor, therapist or healer. It is easy to fall into the trap of believing that we should be able to self-help every imbalance within us. In principle, there may be some truth in this statement but in practice I have yet to meet a therapist who has not needed help from another at some stage. Problems that fall into the category of specific imbalances can range from mild colds to life-threatening illnesses. The more severe the situation, the more necessary it is to seek help.

Many minor conditions, such as burns, cuts or small injuries, respond very well to self-healing techniques. You can do this by holding your hand over or near the damaged part and visualizing the appropriate healing energy flowing into your body. For emotional or psychological problems, you can use imagery exercises, calling upon the relevant archetypal energy from the quantum realm to provide the insights that you need to solve the problem.

The simple guide in assessing the balance of your life is always to look around at what is happening to you or the people closest to you. One of the fundamental principles of being in a physical body is that your outer life is a reflection of what is going on inside. If you are having problems with your boss at work, it is as much an inner problem as an outer one and can be best tackled on an inner level through imagery techniques. You only have to deal with those aspects of your life that are causing a problem at any moment in time. Don't look for problems where there are none, but if they come up try to face them squarely. I know that this can be a hard thing to do, but avoidance will almost always end up causing you more problems in the future.

The more that you maintain an inner balance and deal with any situation that emerges head on, the more fruitful and healthy your life will be. Routine management should therefore be an important aspect of self-healing. This need not be a long, drawn-out process. I always endeavor to spend a few minutes every morning and evening balancing my energies and feeling centered within. You can do this by following the energy balancing exercise in Chapter 2.

In embarking upon a journey of exploration and developing your healing gift, you will connect to many amazing and wonderful parts of yourself. Life is to be lived and it will assuredly bring richness to all that you do. This process will also highlight those aspects of you that need attention, rather like spring sunlight shining through a window after the winter. What looked clean initially now shows much more dirt. We all need to clean and polish our windows continually so that a little bit more sunlight can shine into our lives.

CHAPTER 19

The Quantum Realm

This book is based on three simple ideas:

- First, that there exists a spiritual domain which, like the physical, has a coherent set of principles and laws that links all reality. Interleaved between these two planes is the 'quantum' realm which is accessed through our mind or consciousness. You can do this by using your psychic, or psi, faculty. Evidence of this quantum realm can be found in all cultures on this planet.

- Second, that the 'quantum realm' and the laws that govern it bears many similarities with the internet. With the right knowledge, you can connect your mind to any other person in the world by simply thinking of them. When the link has been made it is then possible to exchange energy or information between you. Telepathy and distant healing are two examples of this energy transfer.

- Third, that fixed into this 'quantum' worldwide web are universities or access points to information, knowledge and wisdom that reflect down from the highest levels of consciousness within this universe. These gateways could be fancifully looked upon as the portals to the gods, who in turn are subject to the supreme intelligence behind reality. Peoples in the past understood this concept and worked with different types of symbolism to gain access to this network. One prime way was to create human or animal images, which were perceived as gods and goddesses representing the essence behind these different universities. These beings could then be invoked, propitiated or called upon by the supplicant. It could be said that Christianity shares this phenomenon in view of the role given to the saints (St Anthony, for example, is invoked when objects have been lost).

All the evidence from mythology and world beliefs points to the existence of eight primary universities in the 'quantum' realm. Each university has a different function covering a broad area of human experience. Within each university, like our university colleges or faculties, there are different departments, which deal with more specific aspects. We can consciously access these universities and their departments through our minds, to draw information that covers all areas of human knowledge. The universities conform to set laws which they will not infringe. Information will only be relayed back to you in line with your inner understanding so that a question posed by a high-ranking scientist would be answered in a different way to a similar question asked by a less experienced student. Prayer is one way to ask for help from these universities. Assistance will always be rendered but it will be assessed in the light of the relevant factors surrounding the situation. Some things can be changed, others cannot. For example, there may be karmic reasons, which your soul accepted when it came into incarnation, which affect a given situation. The principal function of these universities is to help us evolve and grow and this is the prime yardstick against which any request should be made. Asking to win the lottery may not in fact be in your best interests, whereas asking for understanding certainly would be. Like the internet, there is no limitation on the number of requests that you can make. Indeed the greater the amount of connection, the better the channels of communication will be.

Information and help that you obtain can be directed towards the betterment of yourself. It should also have the long-term objective of helping you assist others and the planet as a whole. In the 'quantum' realm, all life is linked into these universities. They are not just for human benefit, but for the welfare of the whole planet. You might like to see them as an expression of Earth's, or Gaia's, consciousness for they help hold all life patterns of the planet in balance.

THE 'QUANTUM' UNIVERSITIES IN THE MODERN WORLD

In most cases today, the knowledge with which these other dimensions can be accessed has been consciously forgotten. Yet these energies are always there and continue to seep out into human consciousness, through symbols and logos. For example, the logo of Bloomsbury Publishing, the original publisher of this work, is a representation of the Roman goddess Diana (the equivalent of the Greek goddess Artemis). Using Figure 19.1 below, you will see that this links with the 'Yellow' university which is to do with grounding ideas in a practical business-like way. In this case the business is publishing books and the symbol is saying that the primary objective of the company is to be a successful business. All companies need an aspect of this same energy in order to survive in today's climate, but a publishing company whose aim is to disseminate particular information might choose a logo that reflected the 'Green' university instead.

Countries in their development also tend to reflect the energies of one or other of these universities. Britain, for example, links very strongly with the 'Violet' university which deals with creative ideas and inventions. The figure of Britannia is a symbol which reflects the image of the Greek goddess Athene. Athene was also a warrior goddess, but she only ever fought to defend. Churchill was able to invoke successfully this spirit in the last war. For the energies of Britain to be properly grounded it needs to be linked to the energy of the 'Yellow' university. In the past, this could be said to have been achieved through the British Empire, and in the future it may be achieved in co-operation with its European partners and with North America. This latter country carries a much closer link to the 'Yellow' university, which is why its star symbol has the five points of the pentangle. However, it is important to remember that while one university may give a predominant flavor to a country's development; all the others are still present and can be accessed as part of that nation's ethos.

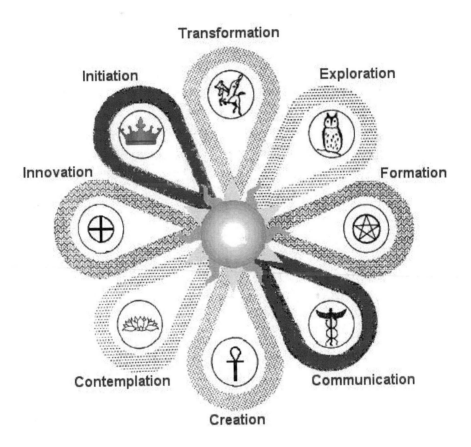

Fig. 19.1 The eight universities of the 'quantum' realm and their key symbols.

INTO THE FUTURE

This book has been an attempt to show you how you can access into the 'quantum' realm using your natural psi abilities. Making these connections could help you take a 'quantum' leap in your own inner development. Indeed, the information and help available to us could solve every problem that at present confronts this planet. In my view, leaders in industry, politicians and all who are in positions of authority need the tools to access this inner world so that the decisions they make are based on wisdom and not fear, folly or greed.

On a personal level, the requirements and challenges of life can all benefit from the extra assistance that comes from the 'quantum' realm. These universities of consciousness cannot lead our lives for us, but they can make them more fruitful.

The keys now lie in your hands; your challenge is to open the door.

Appendix

Heisenberg's Uncertainty Principle Many facets of quantum mechanics give valuable insight into the ways in which psi might operate within us. Heisenberg's Uncertainty Principle states that the harder we try to scrutinize the movements of sub-atomic particles, the more elusive they become. The very act of observing something changes it. Our reality is the product of how we choose to view things. The example of measuring an electron, either in terms of how fast it is moving or its position, demonstrates this notion. By measuring the electron's speed or position we see it either as a wave or a particle. In other words, the electron has the potential of being perceived as either matter (particle) or energy (wave). We perceive its form according to how we choose to measure it.

Heisenberg's *Uncertainty Principle* has led to the development of some startling ideas: reality, at its primary level, is governed not by fixed actualities, but by the possibility of being everywhere and anywhere simultaneously, where both time and space can be reversed and anything might happen. The electron in the first example in its 'virtual state', as it is called, will locate itself simultaneously, in all its potential positions and forms, before dropping back to its original orbit. Time and space are traversed instantaneously.

In Bell's *Theorem* (finally verified by Freedman and Clauser) if a particle is split and the two parts are sent off in different directions, anything that happens to one will instantaneously happen to the other, no matter how far apart they are. This is understood to happen because of a fundamental principle within the universe that requires balance of the whole system. In psi terms, it suggests how we might instantaneously be in contact with and communicate information to another person, simply by thinking of them. This ability has been demonstrated in a number of psi experiments, two of which are included below.

1. **Professor Robert Jahn:** In the 1980s Robert Jahn, an engineering professor at Princetown University, became intrigued with the concept of extending Heisenberg's *Uncertainty Principle,* to see whether the mind could influence events at an atomic level, rather than sub-atomic. To do this he set up a white noise generator from an electrical diode, which is roughly the electronic equivalent of tossing a coin a thousand times a second. Jahn went to great lengths to minimize any interference from the subjects, from equipment failure or bias. Those scientists who have studied his procedures and equipment have been satisfied with the thoroughness of his methodology. In his experiments, subjects were asked to try to make the random generated

line, which is displayed on a monitor, move above or below its datum level, through their mind, by whatever method of visualization or concentration that they chose. To ensure against bias, the subjects had to try to move the line above the set datum for half of the time; and below the line for the other half. As a control, the subjects were asked to sit in the box, leaving it to perform on its own. His first results were published in 1986 after completing a quarter of a million experimental trials. The results showed the subjects' significant ability to produce the desired changes, particularly in some individuals. This would indicate that psi ability, like any artistic gift, is more strongly developed in some individuals than others.

Scientists are still arguing about the results of Jahn's findings. Those that are skeptical about psi have put forward many different explanations involving statistical bias to refute the evidence. Bearing in mind Heisenberg's *Uncertainty Principle* we may never develop a completely foolproof experiment that demonstrates psi. Yet, for its thoroughness, Jahn's is one of the most significant.

2. **Dr Randolph Byrd** In 1987, a remarkable medical study was carried out by Dr Randolph Byrd of the California Medical School in San Francisco, to assess the effectiveness or otherwise of the power of prayer. Over a ten month period, around 400 patients who had been admitted to the coronary care unit for a heart attack or were considered at risk took part in a clinical trial. Half the group received healing 'prayer' treatment, alongside their normal medical care, the other half acted as a control group. The first names of the trial group and a brief sketch of their conditions were handed out to a number of prayer groups throughout the United States.

This was a double blind study, with neither the patients, physicians nor nurses knowing that this study was taking place. Neither was one group sicker than the other. As Dr Larry Dossey, who evaluated the Byrd study in his book *Healing Words*, stated in an article in the American magazine *Body, Mind and Spirit* (August 1994):

'When this meticulous study was concluded it was found that the "prayed-for" group was superior in several ways:
- They were far less likely to develop congestive heart failure.
- They were five times less likely to require antibiotics and three times less likely to require diuretics.
- None of the prayed-for group required an artificial breathing tube, while twelve of the unremembered group required mechanical ventilator support or artificial breathing.
- Fewer of those in the prayed-for group developed pneumonia.
- Fewer of those who had received prayer experienced cardiopulmonary arrest, requiring resuscitation.'

This study clearly shows that prayer can be scientifically evaluated and demonstrates that one human mind can affect another, even in cases where the briefest description of the condition and the forename of patients was the only information given.

Bibliography &
Recommended Reading

Chapter 1: The Psi Function
Where Science and Magic Meet, Serena Roney-Dougal (Element, 1991)
Waking Up, Charles Tart (Shambala, 1986)
The Paranormal, Percy Seymour (Arkana, 1992)
The Nature of Things, Lyall Watson (Hodder & Stoughton, 1990)
The Presence of the Past, Rupert Sheldrake (Fontana, 1989)
Theory of Almost Everything, Robert Barry (Oneworld, 1993)
Wholeness and the Implicate Order, David Bohm (Routledge & Kegan Paul, 1982)
Quantum Healing, Deepak Chopra (Bantam, 1989)
God & The New Physics, Paul Davies (Touchstone, 1983)

Chapter 2: Psi Energy
Your Psychic Power, Carl Rider (Piatkus, 1988)
The Eagle's Quest, Fred Alan Wolf (Thorsons, 1992)
Synchronicity, David Pleat (Bantam, 1987)
The Emperor's New Mind, Roger Penrose (Vintage, 1990)
Natural & Supernatural, Brian Inglis (Prism, 1992)
The Awakened Mind, Max Cade & Nona Coxhead (Wildwood House, 1979)
Life After Life, Raymond Moody (Bantam, 1978)
Return from Death, Margot Grey (Arkana, 1985)
On Death & Dying, Elisabeth Kübler Ross (Tavistock, 1970)
The Tibetan Book of the Dead, translated by Robert Thurman (Aquarian, 1994)
Other Lives, Other Selves, Roger Woolger (Aquarian, 1994)
Twenty Cases Suggestive of Reincarnation, Ian Stevenson (University Press, Charlottesville, 1974)
Many Lifetimes, Denis Kelsey & Joan Grant (1967

Chapter 3: Psi Protection
The Psychic Protection Handbook, Caitlin Matthews (Piatkus 2005)
Subtle Body, Tansley (Thames & Hudson, 1977)
Psychic Self-Defence, Dion Fortune (Thorsons, 1994)
A Handbook of Psychic Protection, Draja Mickaharic (Rider, 1993)
Practical Techniques of Psychic Self-Defence, Murry Hope (Aquarian, 1993)

Chapter 4: Psi Receptivity and Meditation

Are You Psychic, Julie Soskin (Carol and Brown Ltd, 1997)
Channelling for Everyone, Tony Neate (Piatkus, 1997)
The Sixth Sense, Laurie Nadel (Prion, 1991)
How to Meditate, Lawrence LeShan (Thorsons, 1993)
The Silent Path, Michael Eastcott (Rider, 1975)
The Three Minute Meditator, David Harp (Piatkus, 1993)
Increase Your Energy, Louis Proto (Piatkus, 1991)
Meditation in a Changing World, William Bloom (Gothic Image, 1987)

Chapter 5: The Universities of the Mind

The Encyclopaedia of Traditional Symbols, J. C. Cooper (Thames & Hudson, 1978)
Symbolic & Mythological Animals, J. C. Cooper (Aquarian, 1992)
Illustrated Encyclopaedia of Myths and Legends, Arthur Cotterell (Cassell, 1989)
New Larousse Encyclopedia of Mythology (Hamlyn, 1994)

Chapter 6: Working with Your Dreams

Understanding Dreams, Nerys Dee (Thorsons, 1991)
Dictionary for Dreamers, Tom Chetwynd (Aquarian, 1972)
The Lucid Dreamer, Malcolm Godwin (Element, 1994)
Working With The Dreaming Body, Arnold Mindell (Routledge & Kegan Paul, 1985)
The Dream Book, Betty Bethards (Element, 1995)

Chapter 7: The Tools of the Trade

The Silva Mind Control Method, Jose Silva (Granada, 1977)

Chapter 8: Visual Images and Intuition

Knowing Your Intuitive Mind, Dale Olsen (Crystalline Publications, USA, 1990)
Clairvoyant Reality, Lawrence LeShan (Thorsons, 1978)

Chapter 10: Dowsing and Kinesiology

Dowsing, Tom Williamson (Robert Hale, 1993)
Practical Dowsing, A.H. Bell (Bell & Sons, 1965)
The Elements of Dowsing, Henry de France (Bell & Sons, 1977)
The Diviner's Handbook, Tom Graves (Aquarian, 1986)

Chapter 11: Numerology

Your Days Are Numbered, Florence Campbell (Devorss, 1987)
Mark Gruner's Numbers of Life, Mark Gruner & Christopher Brown (Taplinger, N.Y., 1978)
What Number are You, Lila Bek & Robert Holden (Aquarian, 1992)

Chapter 12; Reading the Runes
The Book of Runes, Ralph Blum (Guild Publishing, 1985)
Discover Runes, Tony Willis (Aquarian, 1986)
Using the Runes, Jason Cooper (Aquarian, 1987)

Chapter 13: I Ching
I Ching, translated by Richard Wilhelm (Routledge & Kegan Paul, 1968)
The Illustrated I Ching, R.L. Wing (Aquarian, 1982)
I Ching, Martin Palmer, Jay Ramsay and Xhao Xiaomin (Thorsons, 1995)

Chapter 14: Other Systems of Divination
Step by Step Tarot, Terry Donaldson (Thorsons, 1995)
The Merlin Tarot, R.J. Stewart (Aquarian, 1988)
Tarot, The Complete Guide, Cynthia Giles (Robert Hale, 1992)
The Twelve Houses, Howard Sasportas (Aquarian, 1985)
Astrology, Joan Hodgson (White Eagle Publishing Trust, 1978)
Transpersonal Astrology, Errol Weiner (Element, 1991)
Olympus Self Discovery Cards, Murry Hope (Aquarian, 1991)
Russian Fortune Telling Cards, Svetlana Touchkoff (Harper, 1992)

Chapter 15: Manifesting Your Reality
Living Magically, Gill Edwards (Piatkus, 1991)
The Magic of Believing, Claude Bristol (Pocket Books, 1948)
Applied Visualization, James Page (Quantum, 1990)
Think and Grow Rich, Napoleon Hill (Wilshire Book Company, 1966)

Chapter 16: The Power to Heal
Healing Words, Larry Dossey (Harper Collins, 1993)
Healing Research, Daniel Benor (Helix Verlag, 1993)

Chapter 17: Developing Your Healing Potential
The Healer Within, David Furlong (Piatkus, 1999)
Healing Your Ancestral Patterns David Furlong (Piatkus 1997)
New Dimensions in Healing, Tony Neate (Eye of Gaza Press, 2007)
Hands of Light, Barbara Ann Brennan (Bantam, 1988)
Light Emerging, Barbara Ann Brennan (Bantam, 1993)
Your Healing Power, Jack Angelo (Piatkus, 1994)
I Fly Out With Bright Feathers, Allegra Taylor (Fontana, 1987)
Spiritual Healing, Alan Young (DeVorss, 1981)

Glossary

Archetypes: The primary principles or energies which are linked into the 'collective unconscious' and embody powerful forces in the psyche.

Aura: The composite, subtle fields that surround all life forms. These energy fields lie outside the electro-magnetic spectrum and include emotional, mental and spiritual forces. The aura is sometimes seen clairvoyantly as swirling colors of light.

Bi-location: The ability of consciousness to be in two places at the same time. An individual may actually be seen in two different places at identical times.

Clairaudience: The ability to hear information, either audibly or as an inner voice or sound that conveys information not available to the physical senses.

Clairsentience: The ability to feel sensations within the body, conveying information not available to the physical senses. An example of this might be a healer feeling pain in part of their own body that corresponds with the area of the patient's problem, without the patient having first conveyed this information.

Clairvoyance: The ability to see things from other dimensions not apparent to the physical senses. This can include mental images (with eyes either open or closed) conveying information not otherwise available.

Chakras: Vortices of energy along the front of the body that connect the spiritual realm to the physical. There are seven main chakras in the Hindu tradition, located as follows: top of the head (Crown); between and slightly above the eyes (Brow); throat (Throat); chest (Heart); solar plexus (Solar Plexus); abdomen (Sacral); base of spine (Root).

Ch'i: Chinese word for the subtle energy of the cosmos which provides form and sustenance to the manifest world. This energy can be manipulated to an extent by conscious thought.

Collective unconscious: A Jungian term denoting an energy field that links all human consciousness together. Most individuals are unaware of this interlinking field. In this book it has been likened to the Internet.

De-linking: The reverse of linking (see linking).

Disease (Dis-ease): Disharmony or conflict at any level between, or within, the different elements that link the physical to spiritual body. This principle applies to all life forms, but in human beings it is broadly seen in terms of the physical, emotional, mental and spiritual aspects of our make-up.

Distant healing: The projection of healing energy (Ch'i) to someone or something not present with the healer.

Dowsing: A method of obtaining information using either a pendulum, divining rod or other implement which magnifies the subtle sensations of the physical body.

Dualism: The philosophical notion of two distinct principles existing in all things. Similar to the concept of Yin/Yang but generally carrying an idea that one concept is opposed to the other, like good and bad or light and dark. In human beings, it is thought that the mind or soul and the physical body are two separate entities which are often in conflict with each other.

Ego mind (ego consciousness): The aspect of self, aware of its individuality that has a consciousness, and reflects the different elements, of the physical world. It therefore tends to respond more easily to the needs and appetites of the physical and emotional self as opposed to the spiritual self.

Emotions: Strong feelings including for example joy, sadness, anger, hate, fear or love, for example.

Energy: A force that has an ability to produce an effect on whatever it is directed towards.

Feng Shui: Literally 'wind' and 'water'. Relates to the Chinese notion of being able to balance the Ch'i (or energy) of a place by the correct orientation of buildings, rooms, furniture etc.

Four elements: Traditionally recognized, in many cultures, as four principles that weave through all aspects of the formative and manifest world. At a physical level these are earth, air, fire and water. Within human beings these relate to the four principles of sensation, feeling, thinking and intuition, or the four humours of sanguine, choleric, phlegmatic or melancholic.

Healer: One who consciously projects healing energy or attempts to bring harmony and balance to another individual.

Healing: The process of adjusting energy balances within the body in the search for wholeness or balance. This can either be experienced within the self or projected towards another.

Higher self: The aspect of the spiritual self that is directly in touch with the spiritual realm as opposed to the soul which is the aspect of the spiritual self connected with the mind and body.

Hypnotism: A process of trance induction that bypasses some aspects of the 'ego mind' in order to gain access to the deeper layers within the self.

I Ching: Literally the 'Book of Changes', which is an ancient Chinese text that is the source of Confucian and Taoist philosophy. It is based on the concept that eight primary principles are found in all aspects of life. The combination of these principles gives sixty-four hexagrams forming a divinatory oracle and giving insights into the spiritual forces in operation around the question asked by an individual, helping them make the correct decision.

Individuation process: A Jungian term, expressing the process of connecting the spiritual self with the 'ego mind' so that they act in unison. In this way, the person becomes more aware of themselves as a unique and whole individual.

Inner knowing: An aspect of intuition where the individual, making a connection with their spiritual self, inwardly knows something to be true without any rational or logical explanation for it.

Internet: The computer-based information highway that has links across the world. Ideas and information can be exchanged almost instantly through this network or 'world-wide web'.

Intuition: Immediate mental comprehension without using the process of reasoning.

Jing: Ancestral energy expressed both through sexual release and genetic coding.

Kabala: A mystical system of knowledge that stemmed from Judaic belief. It was originally handed down from teacher to pupil through secret oral instruction.

Karma: The Hindu and Buddhist belief based on the law of cause and effect. Over the span of a number of lives, the results or deeds of one life set the pattern for what happens in the next.

Kwan-Yin: The Chinese goddess of mercy.

Law of Polarities: *see* Yin/Yang.

Life force: The energy from the soul or spiritual essence that gives life to an individual, creature or plant. Death occurs when this energy field de-links from the body.

Linking: The conscious attempt to create an inner connection through the mind, with another person or life form (such as a tree or animal) or to an energy field from the quantum realm. For example, in healing, a mental connection will be made with the client as well as the source of the healing energy.

Lotus posture: A cross-legged posture used in Hatha Yoga where the instep of the foot rests on the opposite thigh.

Mantra: A word that is repeated either audibly or inwardly as part of meditation discipline.

Meditation: A generic word covering a wide range of mental methods of connecting to the inner source of our being.

Metaphor An idea or visual image used in place of another to suggest a likeness between them.

Mind: An aspect of the self that is the seat of conscious and sub-conscious awareness. It links the spiritual self and the emotions.

Morphic Resonance: A concept postulated by biologist Rupert Sheldrake which holds that memories or habits of nature are communicated within species and across generations. This information is held within a 'morphogenic field' which surrounds and links all living things together.

Mudras: A system of inner development based on holding the hands in set positions. These poses create a resonant energy that links different aspects of the self.

Near Death Experience (NDE): An experience reported by those people who have been on the threshold of life and death but may also sometimes happen spontaneously. Part of the consciousness appears to detach itself from the body and is aware of what is taking place from a perspective separate from the body. Sometimes these individuals will then feel they are travelling through a tunnel into another dimension and often report meeting others who they know have already died.

NLP: Neuro-linguistic programming is the art and science of auditory, visual and sensory communication founded by John Grinder and Richard Bandler. It is based on a study of three famous therapists (Milton Erikson, Virginia Satir and Fritz Perls). NLP tries to reframe the way that we think about our reality to bring about change.

Noble Middle Path: A tenet of Buddhism of seeking a balance between extremes.

Past-Life Therapy: A system of healing that seeks to bring relief to behavioral patterns, stemming from a past life experience.

Personality types: A method of categorizing human emotional and behavioral characteristics under a number of headings. At its simplest level it classes individuals as either introverted or extroverted.

Prayer: A verbal request (either outward or inward) for help or intercession from a higher being or deity.

Precognition: Information gathered, through some aspect of psi, about an event in the future which then takes place. Dreams sometimes have a pre-cognitive element.

Psyche: From the Greek meaning 'breath' and refers to the human soul or inner motivating life force.

Psychic or psi faculty: Innate human skill which allows us to communicate and experience different levels of perception outside time or space.

Psychic diagnosis: A way of using the psychic faculty to gain insights and information not apparent to the five physical senses.

Psycho-kinetic: The ability of the mind to influence physical objects, causing them to move or change in ways outside the known laws of physics.

Quantum realm: The threshold between the physical and non-physical world.

Quantum universities: Energy fields within the quantum realm that link through to sources of information and spiritual power.

Regression: An induced state (either by oneself or another person) accessing beyond the conscious mind.

Reincarnation: The belief that each soul lives a number of separate and distinct lives.

Resistance: Anything that causes a barrier to the flow of energy.

Resonance: A concept that explains how energy is transferred between things or people on both a physical and non-physical level. It is based on the notion that, when two objects are pitched musically at the same frequency, energy is exchanged between them. A physical example of this is the radio receiver whose dial has to be adjusted to pick up different stations.

Runes: An ancient Norse and Teutonic magical alphabet used for divination and casting spells.

Sephiroth: The archetypal forms, sometimes seen as attributes of God, which form the basis of the Kabala.

Sexual centre: The base chakric energy centre of the body *(see* chakras).

Shaman: A word that has recently taken on a wide meaning. Originally referring to the 'magician spirit healers' of Finland and Central Asia, it is now applied to all individuals who espouse similar beliefs. One of the main magical symbols of the shaman is the drum which is used to summon up spiritual energy or spirit beings.

Shen: The 'spirit' in Taoist and ancient Chinese belief.

Soul: The aspect of the spirit that directly links into the body.

Spirit: The eternal divine part of the self that contains the sum total of all individual experiences, whether from this life or previous ones.

Spiritual self: Another way of describing the 'spirit' *(see* above).

Tao: Meaning 'The Way'. It is derived from Ancient Chinese and Taoist belief to mean the 'way of right action'. This would be interpreted through the I Ching and was dependent upon prevailing situations of the time. In all cases the individual would try to ally themselves with the highest human and moral principles.

Tarot: A divinatory system based on seventy-eight cards that are divided into a Major Arcana of twenty-two cards and a Minor Arcana of fifty-six cards.

Telepathy: The ability of the mind to communicate directly with another mind across space and time.

Theosophical Society: A metaphysical philosophical society founded by Madam Blavatsky in 1875. It espoused many eastern concepts such as reincarnation, but is perhaps best known for its doctrine of the Masters, who are claimed to be high initiates looking after the development of the world.

Third Eye Center: The brow or Ajna chakric center *(see* chakras).

Transcendental Meditation (TM): A system of meditation introduced into the West by Maharishi Mahesh Yogi in the 1960s based on the repetition of a mantra *(see* mantra).

Vesica Pisces: An important geometrical symbol of two interlocking circles of equal size, where the centre of one circle falls on the circumference of the other. This symbol was a cornerstone of sacred geometry and used extensively in Gothic architecture.

Yin/Yang: Ancient Chinese concept where everything in the manifest world is based upon the interplay of two forces that are at once opposite and complementary. Yang is the outgoing principle whereas Yin is receptive.

Yoga: The word is derived from the Sanskrit and means 'union'. Generally this is taken to mean 'union with the spiritual self'. There are many different schools of Yoga of which the best known, in the West, is Hatha Yoga which works with different body postures to attain higher states of consciousness.

Yogi: The term for an Indian holy man who follows one of the traditional systems of yoga.

Useful Addresses

COURSES IN PSI DEVELOPMENT AND HEALING

UNITED KINGDOM

David Furlong and Atlanta Association
'Myrtles'
Como Road, Malvern
Worcestershire WR14 2TH
T.   +44(0)1684 569105
E.   atlanta@dial.pipex.com
W.   www.atlantaassociation.com/

British Society of Dowsers
2 St Ann's Road,
Malvern,
Worcestershire.
WR14 4RG, UK. T.
T.   +44 (0)1684 576969
E.   info@britishdowsers.org
W.   www.britishdowsers.org

College of Healing
PO Box 568,
Banbury,
Oxon
OX16 6AW
T.   + 44 (0) 1295 264141
E.   Collegeofhealing@aol.com
W.   www.collegeofhealing.org

The College of Psychic Studies
16 Queensbury Place,
London SW7 2EB
T.   +44 (0)20 7589 3292
E.   admin@collegeofpsychicstudies.co.uk/
W.   www.collegeofpsychicstudies.co.uk

Edinburgh College of Parapsychology
2 Melville Street
Edinburgh
EH3 7NS
T.   +44 (0)131 220 1433
E.   secretary@parapsychology.org
W.   www.parapsychology.org.uk/

Findhorn Foundation
The Park
Findhorn
IV36 3TZ
T.   +44 (0)1309 690311
E.   enquiries@findhorn.org
W.   www.findhorn.org

The National Federation of Spiritual Healers
Old Manor Farm Studio
Church Street, Sunbury-on-Thames
Middlesex
TW16 6RG
T.   +44 (0)1932 783164
W.   www.nfsh.org.uk

The White Eagle Lodge
New Lands,
Brewells Lane, Rake
Liss, Hampshire
GU33 7HY
T.   +44 (0)1730 893300
E.   info@whiteagle.org
W.   www.whiteagle.org

Spirit Release Foundation
'Myrtles', Como Road
Malvern
Worcestershire
WR14 2TH
T.   +44 (0) 1684 560725
E.   spiritrelease@dsl.pipex.com
W.   www.spiritrelease.com

All correspondence regarding training courses run by David
Furlong should be sent to Atlanta Association at the address given on
page 205.

Index